STUFF
GUYS
NEED
TO
KNOW

STUFF GUYS
NEED TO KNOW

How to Do Just About Everything

John F. Hunt

CITADEL PRESS
Kensington Publishing Corp.
www.kensingtonbooks.com

CITADEL PRESS books are published by

Kensington Publishing Corp.
850 Third Avenue
New York, NY 10022

All Kensington titles, imprints, and distributed lines are available at special quantity discounts for bulk purchases for sales promotions, premiums, fund-raising, educational, or institutional use. Special book excerpts or customized printings can also be created to fit specific needs. For details, write or phone the office of the Kensington special sales manager: Kensington Publishing Corp., 850 Third Avenue, New York, NY 10022, attn: Special Sales Department, phone 1-800-221-2647.

Citadel Press and the Citadel logo are trademarks of Kensington Publishing Corp.

First printing October 2001

10 9 8 7 6 5 4 3 2

Printed in the United States of America

Library of Congress Control Number: 2001092648

ISBN 0-8065-2129-5

To my father and brother:

Lee H. Hunt

Thomas C. Hunt

CONTENTS

Part Seven   Don't Try This at Home!
A Crash Course in Emergency First Aid

Part Eight   Goin' to the Chapel:
A Crash Course in Wedding Etiquette

Part Nine   There's No Place Like Home:
A Crash Course in Basic Home Ec

ACKNOWLEDGMENTS

I would like to thank the following people who assisted me, in some way or another, with this book:

Matt Lively, for his illustrations
Stewart McGough
Paul Keller
Chris Hunt
Stephanie Hunt
Evelyn Hunt
Scott Reinhardt
Elly Robinson
Rob Robinson
Linda Robinson
Randy Robinson
Laura White
Denise Bird
Leslie Davis
Jim Brownell

I would like to especially thank my beautiful wife, Wendy Hunt, for her assistance, and for putting up with me when I was writing.

PREFACE

On April 25, 1990, when the Space Shuttle *Discovery* deployed the Hubble space telescope, scientists and astronomers from around the world were hoping to catch a glimpse of unseen solar systems, distant stars, far-away galaxies, supernovas, egg nebulas, and possibly, through their new window to the universe, the two factors which, joined together, would help explain the mystery of our own existence. More than a decade later, NASA has spent over a billion dollars, and probably just as many man-hours trying to discover what two elements had to come together to explain how our crazy world ended up the way it has.

Even though scientists are still trying to unravel this mystery, the question they have recently answered is that there is an enormous amount of "stuff" that men do not know how to do. In a recent poll, 83 percent of men stated that they did not know how to clean a fish; 61 percent were not sure of the exact way to carve a turkey; and 98 percent did not know how to set a table.

After encountering a similar dilemma, I decided to write the book *Stuff Guys Need to Know*. My father did not know how to tie a bow tie, and he unfortunately discovered this only fifteen minutes before he had to be at a black-tie dinner. A few days later, I thought it would be a good idea to find him a book on the subject. To make a long story short, I couldn't find a book on tying a bow tie, or cleaning a fish, or carving a turkey, or setting a table.

So, I wrote this book to help all the guys out there who will never be exposed to situations where they can learn different "stuff." I was lucky enough to have a brother who once lived in Tokyo, so when I was seventeen he taught me how to use chopsticks and decipher a sushi menu. My wife's father and brother happen to be champion fishermen who have set world records. When I was twenty-five they taught me how to clean a fish. *Stuff Guys Need to Know* is a collection of about seventy-five different things that every guy should know how to do, but that very few have ever actually been taught. For every one guy like myself, who has been fortunate enough to learn how to do many different things, I know that there are thousands of others out there who will need a little instruction. Here it is.

PART ONE

Separating the Men From the Boys: A Crash Course in Manly Traditions

1

How to Open a Jar

I think it is safe to say that we have all been in the company of a woman who has passed us a jar to be opened. When it comes to equal rights, some things have been overlooked, and opening a jar is one of the unequal rights left for men to deal with. A secret committee of women probably got together and decided there were a few things they just didn't want to do. Other tasks on the list include finding out what that noise was at 2:00 AM, scooping out the guts of a pumpkin during Halloween, killing spiders, cleaning up dog poop, lubricating the car, removing a hornet's nest, and doing anything involving the use of WD-40.

Step 1. Make sure the jar and your hands are clean. Grease on your hands, as well as grease on the jar, can make you lose your grip. Thoroughly wash and dry your hands and the jar if there is any grease.

Step 2. The best way to open a jar is to use leverage—not just the strength of your hands, but the length of your arms as well. Put the lid of the jar in the web of your dominant hand, between your thumb and index finger. Don't grab the lid on top with the palm of your hand. Don't just work hard, work smart.

Step 3. Hold the jar with your other hand at about chest level, a few inches out in front of you. Don't hold it against your chest. This will prevent you from using your arms.

Step 4. While holding the lid in the web of your dominant hand, and the jar in your other hand, bring the jar into your chest. (If you were a bird, it would look like you are going to flap your wings.) Hold the lid firmly, and twist the jar.

If this doesn't work, try tapping on the edge of the lid with the handle of a butter knife, and go back to Step 1. The tapping will break the vacuum seal holding the lid.

If this doesn't work, try running the lid under very hot water. Lids are made of metal, and the metal will heat up quickly. As the lid heats up, the metal expands, and pulls away from the glass. It will also wash away any sticky goo that could have gotten under the seam. Thoroughly dry your hands and the jar then go back to Step 1.

Rule of Thumb: If you have tried each of these steps three times it is OK to break the jar and forget about it. (Just kidding!)

2

How to Tie Knots

Out of the hundreds of different types of knots, I have chosen to teach you eight. If you learn how to tie these eight, you should be able to live the rest of your life without ever having to learn a new type. If you do come across another type of knot that could not be substituted for one of the following— well, then I guess you will know how to tie nine different types of knots.

1. Driver's Hitch

The driver's hitch (or trucker's knot) should be used when tying heavy loads when a very tight rope is needed. Use this knot if you have to secure a canoe or a mattress to the top of a car.

2. Two Half Hitches

An all-purpose knot. Use it to tie a cord to a tent, or a rope to a tree. I have heard that this is the knot commonly used by the Coyote when he is trying to set a trap for the Roadrunner.

3. The Figure Eight Follow Through

Use this knot to tie two pieces of rope together. The reason I recommend this knot is that it is easier to untie than other knots used to fasten two ropes.

4. The Clove Hitch

Use the clove hitch when you are tying a rope to a pole and you want the knot to tighten and constrict around the pole. This knot can be used to tie ropes to small trees or even to close the top of a garbage bag.

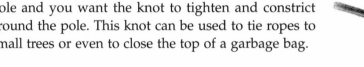

5. The Bowline

The bowline is great for tying objects or animals to something stationary. It is very reliable and is considered the only safe knot if you are tying a rope around the neck of an animal (such as a horse).

6. The Slip Knot

Use this knot when you need to be able to adjust the tension or length of a rope. A good example is if you have to make an adjustment in a tarp that has already been tied down.

7. The Square Knot

The square knot can be used for general bundle tying. It is not a reliable method for tying two ropes together that are under strain as the knot can easily be broken.

8. The Cinch Knot

Use the cinch knot (or clinch knot) to tie fishing line to hooks, lures, swivels, or flies. Place the line through the eye of the hook, double back, make five turns around the standing part of the line, and pass the end of the line through the first loop above the eye of the hook and then through the large loop. Pull on the end of the line and slide the coils down tight against the hook eye.

3

How to Open a Beer Bottle Without Using an Opener

It seems that in the past few years the popularity of microbrewery beer has grown dramatically. I applaud the people who chase the American dream, starting their own business and sharing the fruits of their labors with the citizens of the world. What I don't like about microbreweries is that they have smaller budgets than the larger breweries. Since they have smaller budgets, costs need to be cut. One of the first features that is eliminated is the ever-popular twist-off cap. As the popularity of microbrews grows, so do the odds that you will need a bottle opener.

Step 1. Find the Ideal Place to Open Your Bottle

To open a beer bottle without an opener, find something made of wood that doesn't matter if it gets scratched or chipped. I suggest a wooden fence, a two by four, a picnic table, a log, a tree, etc. Wood is the best substance to use as your opener because it is strong enough to withstand some force, but it will give way before the glass does. You have a lot better chance of breaking your bottle if you attempt this on a metal fence or concrete wall.

Step 2. Positioning the Cap and Bottle

Place the rim of the bottle cap on an edge of the piece of wood you have chosen. While pressing firmly against the rim of the bottle cap, tilt the bottle up at about a 45-degree angle.

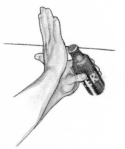

Step 3. Hitting the Cap

Once you have the bottle in place, hit the cap firmly with the palm of your hand in a downward motion. The force of the blow should be enough to separate the bottle cap from the bottle. If the cap doesn't come loose, try again, using a little more force. Repeat until you have succeeded.

4

How to Start a Charcoal Grill

There are few things more pleasurable in life than having a good old-fashioned backyard BBQ. It is an excellent excuse to get friends together and partake of two of my favorite activities: eating and drinking. To do that, however, you have to know how to get the grill going—it's another area where men are still in charge.

What You Will Need

1. A charcoal grill
2. Charcoal briquettes
3. Charcoal-lighter fluid
4. Gloves and apron
5. Heavy duty aluminum foil
6. Tongs
7. Long-handled utensils
8. Hickory chips (for flavor if you're not using hickory charcoal)
9. Outdoor grill thermometer (for meat)
10. A grilling basket (for smaller vegetables)

11. Carving knife and fork
12. A wire brush

Step 1. Preparing the Grill

First, use a wire grill brush to loosen stuck-on food particles, then spray the grate with oven cleaner and rinse thoroughly, or wash with hot soapy water. Prior to grilling, rub the grate with vegetable oil or spray with non-stick cooking spray to prevent food from sticking.

Step 2. Lighting the Fire

If not executed properly, lighting a charcoal grill can be a pain in the ass and will take forever. The first thing you have to do is to make sure the air vent on the bottom of the grill is open and free of any debris (the charcoal will light faster with better air circulation). Next, arrange the charcoal briquettes in a pyramid at the bottom of the grill. Add approximately 3–4 ounces of lighter fluid to the briquettes and carefully light them with a match. No matter how hard a charcoal grill is to light, *never ever* use anything other than lighter fluid, like gasoline, to light your fire. Gasoline is not only dangerous, but it can make your food taste like crap, and even poison you. In about twenty minutes after the flames have died down, the coals will be ready for cooking. A good way to tell when the coals are ready is that if you are grilling during the day the coals will be covered with a gray ash, if you are grilling at night the coals will give off a bright red glow. In any case they will take about 20–30 minutes to be ready for grilling. Plan accordingly. After the coals have properly ignited, using your tongs, spread the briquettes into a single layer or bank them for different heat zones, and set the grilling grid in place.

Step 3. How Do I Tell How Hot the Grill Is?

The best way to tell how hot your grill is by using the hand test. To estimate the temperature hold your hand, palm side down, about six inches away from the coals. Count one thousand one, one thousand two, etc., until the heat becomes too uncomfortable for you to bear. If you have a normal pain threshold, the count should provide an accurate measurement of temperature:

- 2 seconds: Hot, 400 degrees or higher
- 3 seconds: Medium hot, about 350–375 degrees
- 4 seconds: Medium, about 300–350 degrees
- 5 seconds: Low, about 250–300 degrees
- 10 seconds: Light it again.

To lower the temperature either raise the grid or spread out the coals. To raise the temperature lower the grid or move the coals closer together.

Step 4. Put Food on the Grill

Place longer-cooking food on first, then add foods that cook in a shorter interval. Time it so that everything gets done at the same time.

Tips

1. The best way to avoid flare-ups is to place a foil drip tray in between the coals and the grid. (A single sheet of aluminum foil will do. The foil will block the drippings while still conducting heat.) If you have already started grilling and are having flare-ups, either raise the grid, spread out the coals, or remove a few coals. If this still doesn't work, spray a mist of water on the coals, but be careful not to totally put out your fire.
2. Add more coals when the heat has died out, the coals aren't glowing anymore, there is no smoke, or the food is not sizzling anymore. Add them a few at a time; you don't want to smother the glowing coals and cut off the heat.
3. Mix in a few hickory chips (soak them in water first) with the charcoal. Hickory adds a great barbecue flavor to meats. It smells great, too.
4. Use tongs rather than a fork when turning meats. The fork will pierce the meat, causing it to lose juice, dry out, and cause flare-ups.
5. Close the lid and the vents after you are done; this will extinguish the coals safely.
6. After the ashes are cold, dump them in the trash. *Don't* leave them in the grill. If the ashes get damp, they will form lye, which will eat through the metal and ruin your grill.

5

How to Build a Campfire

There are several reasons why you build a campfire. The first reason is because you have decided to go camping with some friends and you want to cook the fish you caught that afternoon. The second reason is that you like to watch the flames and feel the warmth. The third reason is that you are lost in the woods and if you don't build a fire you may freeze to death or possibly never be spotted by the rescue plane. There are a few different types of campfires you can build, but instead of teaching you the differences between them all, I am going to tell you about one that can be used in all situations. Let's hope you never fall into the lost-and-cold category, but if you do, try to be fortunate enough to be carrying matches—preferably waterproof matches.

Step 1. Preparing the Fireplace

When you have found a place where you want to have your campsite, it is time to clear a place to build a fire. Choose a site that is somewhat sheltered (in a valley rather than on top of a hill), especially if it is windy. Do not light a fire under a tree that has overhanging branches. It is possible to either damage the tree, or if it is very dry, to even set the tree on fire. Clear away leaves, twigs, moss, and dry grass from a circle at least six feet across, and scrape everything away until you have a surface of bare earth. Once you have cleared your area, try to find some rocks about the size of a softball to surround the fireplace. The purpose of the rocks is to keep the burning fire within a predetermined area, and it also looks pretty.

Step 2. Gathering Your Fuel

In the woods surrounding your campsite, you are going to have to search for things that you can burn in your fire. There are three categories of fuel:

1. **Tinder**—Tinder is leaves, dry grass, and twigs.
2. **Kindling**—Kindling is small pieces of wood and sticks about a quarter to a half-inch in diameter.
3. **Wood**—Wood should range in size from a half-inch to about six inches in diameter.

Gather as much as you can find (it will burn faster than you think), and make sure it is *dry*. Also, never try to use branches that you have broken off a tree. This wood is called green wood, and will be too wet from its sap to burn.

Step 3. Building the Base

The type of campfire I am teaching you to build is a combination of two structures that will be used together to burn as one. The first thing you need to do it is take four of the larger sticks and make a base for the fire. Lay two sticks down on the ground about 1–1½ feet apart. Take two more sticks and lay them parallel to each other, but overlapping the other two sticks. You will be forming a box, but the sides will overlap and not meet exactly.

Step 4. Tinder and Kindling

Now that you have established the base of the campfire, gather up the tinder and put it into the middle of the box. Don't just throw it there in a loose pile, but take handfuls of the grass and leaves and compact them with your hands. (Into the size of golf balls or baseballs.) Make a pile of these balls in the middle of the box. Next, take the smaller twigs and kindling and build a lean-to tepee that surrounds the tinder.

Step 5. Adding to the Base

Once you have put the tinder and kindling in the middle of the square, it is time to add to the base. Keep adding sticks in the same patterns as the four you put on the ground, but as you continue to add sticks, move them slightly inward. As you add successive layers, bring them closer together. As you do this you will be forming a pyramid. Make sure the pyramid is close to the tinder, as it will become part of the fire. The pyramid you have just built around the lean-to will serve three purposes. First, it will protect the tinder and kindling from any sudden wind gusts, allowing it to catch fire quicker. Second, while adding protection, the gaps in the wood will allow the fire to breathe evenly. *Fires need air to burn,* but not in the form of gusts. Third, the wood will eventually catch fire and burn.

Step 6. Come On, Baby, Light My Fire

If there is any wind, either wait for it to die down a little or position your back to the wind and use your body as a shield. When you are in position, strike a match, and, by placing your fingers through one of the gaps in the base of the pyramid, light the tinder. If there is no wind, and the fire is having a little trouble getting started, try blowing *slowly and steadily* on the base of the fire. The air will help the fire to burn. If all of your kindling, tinder, and wood are dry, you should be able to light a fire with one match.

Step 7. Keeping the Fire Going

As the fire begins to burn the tinder and then the pyramid, you are going to have to keep adding fuel to keep it going. Once the fire has established itself, start placing the larger pieces of wood on the fire. Start by leaning the larger pieces of wood against the pyramid, like the tepee you built with the smaller sticks on the inside. Keep adding as necessary, but make sure there is adequate space between the logs for air.

Step 8. Putting It Out

Whatever you do before you leave the campsite, *make sure your fire is completely out,* and I mean *completely.* The best way to do it, if you have any spare water, or if you are camping near a river, is to drench the campfire with as much water as possible. If you don't have a lot of water available, then pee on the fire. It will work just as well. It is also recommended that you throw dirt on the coals. However, all dirt is not created equal, make sure that the dirt doesn't contain leaves and twigs, for they can be fuel that restarts the fire. When you think the fire is out, scrape at the coals with a stick and put your hand over them to see if you can feel any heat. It is possible for campfires to smolder for hours and eventually relight, and that, my friend, is one way that forest fires start.

6

How to Negotiate

I wanted to include "How to Negotiate" in this book because when I was eighteen I bought my first new car and I got ripped off. It was not a glamorous sports car, but a used Honda Civic, which happened to be something I could afford. I had done some research on the car, knew what to look for and how much to spend, but what I didn't take into consideration was how my emotions were going to make me act. At the time, Honda Civics were very popular and it was hard to locate one that I could afford. After weeks of what seemed like useless searching, I finally found the car I wanted. It was in a no-name, out-of-the-way used car lot and there was only one left. The price was a little out of my range, but all the salesman had to say was that he had someone coming by tomorrow to look at it, and the next thing I knew, I was driving home in a "new" car. After a few weeks, when the newness of the car had worn off, I realized that I paid about a thousand dollars too much. What I didn't realize at the time was that when I first saw the car, the emotional side of my brain had taken over the rational side. It didn't matter what the car cost, I wanted it, I was sick of looking all over town, I had to have it. I freaked out and just bought it. I am sure it was the easiest sale that salesman had ever made. I didn't even attempt to negotiate with him.

The ironic thing is that when I sold that same car it was to a sixteen-year-old kid, who luckily brought his father with him to look at it. The father was calm, cool, and collected, and he talked me down the few hundred dollars that I built into the price. (Which I anticipated, so I advertised the car at $500 dollars more than I was actually prepared to take for it.) The kid, on the other hand, was the exact opposite. (Actually he reminded me of myself when I bought the car years ago.) He was going berserk. All he said was "Dad, this is it, this is it! This is the one I want! This is it!" I thought he was having some type of spasm and might start to foam at the mouth. Finally, his embarrassed father told him to calm down and go sit in their car. I knew that if the kid had come by himself I could have easily sold him the car without taking off the built-in negotiation money. Although the following is a brief introduction to negotiation, and the subject could take up thousands of pages, I think that it is extremely important that everyone should be familiar with the fundamentals.

Not every negotiation you engage in will be the same, nor can negotiations be scripted or predicted. A negotiation may be between you and a close friend or you and a complete stranger; some will be cut-and-dried, yes-or-no-type problems, while others will cover several issues, each of which could be solved differently. A negotiation could be between two people or it could be among several people; every one will have its own personality. Even though there are several often uncontrollable variables that need to be taken into consideration when negotiating, the two aspects you have some direct control over are yourself and your emotions.

The most important aspect of negotiation is preparation. If you enter into a negotiation not knowing the outcome you want, you will "lose" every time. You have to have a specific goal in mind, but realize that the other party involved also has his own agenda, and it will rarely be the same as yours. You have to be willing to make concessions, or at least give the appearance of doing so. You also have to realize the possibility that you will walk away empty-handed.

Prior to entering into your next negotiation, take a few minutes and consider the following variables. Some may not directly apply to your situation, but each will give you a good place to start and help you figure out your priorities. Take into consideration the following factors when negotiating. For illustration purposes I will use the example of purchasing a new car.

Negotiation Preparations

1. The Bottom Line What exactly do you want?

- Have you prioritized what is important to you?
- Do you understand the other side of the story?
- What is it that you want most?
- What is the purpose of your want?

- For example, do you *want* or *need* a new car? Do you want a sports car for status, or do you need basic transportation?

2. Options Do you have a one-sided focus?

■ What points do you agree upon?
■ Will someone "win" and someone "lose" in this negotiation?
■ Are your interests compatible?

■ For example, I agreed to pay full price for the car, since the owner was willing to throw in carpeted floors and alloy wheels.

3. Alternatives Can I walk away from the current situation?

■ Do you think you/they are getting a fair deal?
■ Do you know how the other party will react if you end the negotiation?
■ Does one person have an upper hand?

■ For example, this is the exact car I want and there is only one left. However, the price is $2,000 too high, and the seller is not willing to come down. Should I walk away from the deal?

4. Fairness Are you getting ripped off?

■ Are you being treated unfairly?
■ Will I have to explain my actions to my friends and family?
■ Are your emotions overshadowing reality?

■ For example, if you agree to buy the new car at the asking price, is it a good deal?

5. Point of View Do you understand the other party's situation? Does that party understand your situation?

■ Does the other party know what you are looking for?
■ Are you being sold something you don't need?
■ Are you having a two-way conversation?

■ For example, I told the car salesman that I wanted leather seats, so why is he showing me cars without them?

6. Consequences What will the effect of our negotiation be?

■ Will it affect a personal relationship?
■ Will I put myself in a difficult situation if I don't agree or solve the problem with the other party?
■ Is the person I am dealing with the actual problem?

■ For example, if I agree to buy this new car at the asking price, can I afford the monthly payments?

7. Follow-Through What can I expect of this agreement?

- Will the other party follow through with his end of the deal?
- Can I live up to my end of the agreement?
- Am I negotiating with the decision-maker?

- For example, this car salesman is quoting me a great price, but will his sales manager allow him to sell the car at such a low price?

What to Say

OK, now that you have those seven important preparation points in mind, what's next? Whatever you are going to buy, *find out what the going price is.* For a new car, check out a few lots and see what their prices are, or check out prices on the Internet. For used cars find out the *Blue Book* value. To negotiate you have to have a *realistic* idea of the price.

So, just exactly what do you say when you negotiate? If you are buying a new car, *after* you test drive it, return to the lot, and agree that you like the car, the first thing you say is, "How much is this car going to cost?" Generally, the salesman will quote the dealer's (not the manufacturer's) sticker price posted on (what else?) a sticker on the window. (Some dealers will build in unrealistic added costs; that's why you have to research several dealers first.) You then counter with "No, what is this car *really* going to cost me?" The salesman will see that you are truly interested and are willing to deal. Generally, depending on the number of options (the more options, the greater the latitude to deal), he will come down in price, but not by a lot. You then give him a counteroffer (deduct 10 percent of the price). He will probably not accept your counteroffer, but you should be able to come to a price somewhere between the offer and counteroffer. Please understand that most salesmen are not empowered to make deals involving deep discounts; the salesman will most likely call in a sales manager to finish negotiating with you. Don't be upset or alarmed over this; it is the normal way things are handled at a car dealership.

For a used car, inspect the car thoroughly and note every flaw (every used car has some). Test drive the car, note any peculiarities, and tell the owner what they are while you're driving. If you're satisfied that the car is essentially sound, you can start negotiating. Remember, every used car will require some amount of repair or maintenance replacement of parts; this will allow you to negotiate a lower price. First, establish the asking price; then point out to the owner that it will cost you money to fix whatever flaws the car has. At this point, make him a counteroffer. If he doesn't accept your offer and makes no counterproposal, ask him to come back with a price. Both of you should be able to reach an agreement somewhere in between your two offers.

Not just cars, but the price of most items can be negotiated. The higher the mark-up on the item the more leeway there is in negotiation (for example, jewelry and clothing have a high mark-up from wholesale to retail prices). Also, if you are willing to spend more money (for example, if you want to buy a couple of hundred dollars' worth of CDs), the owner or manager of a store may be willing to come down in price from the retail tag. Negotiation requires that the dealer makes a profit and that you get a fair price. Try it, you'll like it.

7

How to Choose a Cigar

There are two basic rules about cigars: You are either a cigar smoker or you are not a cigar smoker.

That's basically it. However, I will expand on that thought to help you get a better picture of what I am talking about. A cigar smoker is a person who will smoke anything in a brown wrapper with a diameter bigger than a finger. If you wrapped an expensive cigar in white paper and offered it to a "cigar smoker" he would probably say, "No, I don't smoke." Cigar smokers usually don't consider themselves to be smokers. They think smokers are people who smoke cigarettes. (This is like saying, "Sure, I do drink a case of beer a day, but it is light beer, so I am not an alcoholic.") They are a different breed. But it does help to explain why cigar smokers don't understand why people complain about the smell when they light up.

If you are not a cigar smoker, then, basically, you have not had a good cigar or don't smoke at all. I consider myself a non-cigar smoker, but there was one occasion when I had to go to a business dinner after which the host offered me a cigar. Since the man was a big client of the company I was working for and I did not want to offend him, I smoked it. I thought it was going to taste like licking an ashtray, but it was actually very good and I enjoyed it. The trick is picking a good one. Since a good cigar is a matter of taste, the best way to find one you like is to try new varieties until you smoke one that appeals to you in a big way.

There are no clear rules that define cigars. As a result, a cigar company may have its own definitions and classifications. Basically, what this means is that if you bought a *Robusto* or a *Culebra* from Company A it will probably not be the same as a *Robusto* or *Culebra* from Company B. Even though there is a lot of variation from one manufacturer to another, there are general classifications that will help you make your selection.

Cigar Classifications

Cigarillo Looks like, and is, the size of a cigarette. Ring gauge of less than 29.

Demitasse Slightly bigger than a cigarillo. Ring gauge of 30.

Panatela A medium cigar. About 5 or more inches. Ring gauge of 34–39.

Culebra Also a medium cigar, however it is braided. About 5½–6 inches. Ring gauge of 39.

Petit Corona Shorter and not as thick as a Corona. Under 5 inches. Ring gauge of 40–44.

Corona A thick, straight cigar. About 5 inches. Ring gauge of 42.

Double Corona Basically a longer Corona. About 6 inches. Ring gauge of 50.

Grand Corona Thick and smooth. About 5½–6½ inches. Ring gauge of 45–47.

Robusto A short, thick cigar. About 4½ inches. Ring gauge of 48–50.

Churchill (As in Winston.) About 6–8 inches. Ring gauge of more than 50.

Pyramid-Torpedo (the Mack Daddy) Long, thick, and tapered at both ends. About 6½ inches or more. Ring gauge of 60. GRRRRRRR!

Cigar Strength

There are basically four classifications for cigar strength: mild, mild to medium, medium to full-bodied, and full-bodied (not rocket science).

Ring Gauge and Length

The ring gauge is the thickness of a cigar. It is measured in sixty-fourths of an inch; for example, 44 is the diameter of a dime, 48, a nickel, and 54, a quarter. The thicker the cigar, or larger the ring gauge, the fuller the flavor. Thinner cigars have a harder time holding their flavor. (It is also rumored that apprentices learn the art of cigar rolling with the smaller cigars. Most cigar aficionados therefore prefer larger cigars.) There is no relation between ring gauge and length, and the only thing "cigar length" means is that it will last longer.

Cigar Construction

There are three main components of a cigar. The bunch (or filler), the binder, and the wrapper. Filler is the individual tobacco leaves that are used in the body of a cigar, which can be composed of up to four different types of tobacco. (Cheap filler uses scraps and trimmings.) This blended tobacco is called the bunch. The binder is the part of a tobacco leaf that is used to hold the bunch together. Finally, what most people consider the most important part of the cigar, is the wrapper. Basically it is a tobacco leaf wrapped around the bunch and binder that holds the whole thing together in a nice, manly package.

Types of Cigar Wrappers

Candela or Double Claro A bright green to greenish brown shade of wrapper. Used in wrapping less expensive cigars. Its greenish color is a result of cost-cutting in the manufacturing process: To save money, companies often like to do things in bulk. In this case, the tobacco is heat-cured in some giant warehouse, and the green color comes from the chlorophyll in the leaves. There is nothing better than a bright green cigar and a nice warm glass of sour milk. Mmmmmm! (I hope you understand I'm joking!)

Claro or Natural Tan. Very popular with teens and vagrants.

English Market Selection (EMS) Preferred in the English market. A little richer than a Claro and tan to medium brown.

Colorado Claro Medium brown color.

Colorado Reddish brown to dark brown.

Colorado Maduro Rich dark brown.

Maduro Very dark brown to almost black.

Oscuro Black and very strong.

Country of Tobacco Origin and Tobacco Characteristics

The strength of a cigar is based upon, well, basically, the type and strength of tobacco in it. There are no clear-cut characteristics that apply to each country where the tobacco is grown, but here are a few general characteristics.

Brazil Spicy, strong

Canary Islands Mild to medium

Cuba Medium to full-bodied

Dominican Republic Mild

Ecuador Mild

Honduras Spicy, full-bodied

Jamaica Mild (everyt'ing is mild in Jamaica, mon)

Mexico Mild to harsh

Nicaragua Mild to medium

United States Mild

Cigar Storage

If you are like myself and not a big smoker, try to smoke cigars as soon as possible after you buy them. If not, they should be kept in a humidor. Don't try to keep them in a drawer, shoe box, or refrigerator. They will only dry out, and smoking a dry cigar is like smoking a paper bag. Humidors need to be kept at 70–72 percent relative humidity and have a temperature of 70°F. A humidor is basically a sealed environment that keeps both of these elements stable. Try to avoid rapid fluctuation in either one. Also, see your local cigar retailer to learn more about cigars and humidors.

8

How to Hold a Baby

There are two reasons I decided to include "How to Hold a Baby" in this section. The first reason is simple: Women find it incredibly sexy when a man holds a baby! (Hold a baby in the presence of a woman and you will understand what I am talking about.)

The second reason is a little more selfish. Research has shown that the more babies are held, the quicker they will meet their "contact quota." The quicker this quota is met, the better chance the child will be one who doesn't cry too much, isn't clingy or dependent, or, in a nutshell, won't be a pain in the ass. Also, the more a baby is held, the less I have to hear it crying when I am trying to eat my dinner.

So ultimately, the more you hold a baby, especially if it's yours, the better chance you will have to raise a well-adjusted, intelligent, non-pain-in-the-ass child. If you can do that, as far as I am concerned, you have done one of the manliest things I can think of.

When my niece was born, she only weighed 4 pounds 13 ounces—a little sucker. She was so small that I was scared senseless that she would break if I held her the wrong way. When it was my turn to hold her, I held her in an uncomfortable position, and, of course, it only took a few seconds before she started to cry. A nurse once told me that you do have to remember to be gentle with babies, but you also have to hold them securely. They are just like dogs and know when you are afraid. (Ever notice that babies always cry when they are held by one particular person, but they instantly stop when they are held by another?)

There are two basic ways to hold a baby:

The Traditional Cradle

Newborn babies like to snuggle and hear the comforting rhythm of your heartbeat. The traditional cradle is done when the baby's body is facing yours and his head is turned sideways. Use one hand to support the baby's neck and the other to hold his bottom. The traditional cradle hold helps babies drift off to sleep.

The Sitting Position

The sitting position is where you support the baby's back with your forearms and hold his head in your hands (with his legs resting against your chest). This allows you and the baby to see eye to eye.

9

How to Burp a Baby

Pointers

1. Remember, babies are very fragile little people. There is no need to bang on their backs in order to elicit a burp. Remember when you were small and the school bully pushed you around, how big and strong you thought he was? Well, multiply that by 1,000 and that is you. Be gentle!

2. Also it is also very important to support the baby's neck and head. The neck muscles are very weak. Do not let the head flop forward or backward.
3. *Never* shake a baby.
4. On the flip-side of the coin, don't worry about breaking the baby. Use your common sense. Be gentle but firm when holding a baby. They are fragile, but they need support, too.

What You Will Need

1. A baby
2. A soft cloth you don't mind getting puke on.

Three Basic Ways to Burp a Baby

On the Shoulder

Step 1. Drape the cloth over your shoulder.

Step 2. Hold the baby firmly against your shoulder. Support the baby by putting your arm or hand under his bottom.

Step 3. Gently rub and pat the baby's back. If this does not work, repeat, but with a little more force. The key phrase of that sentence is "a *little* more." Use your common sense.

Lying Down

Step 1. Place the cloth in your lap.

Step 2. Place the baby in your lap on his stomach facing down. The stomach should be on one thigh and the head should be supported by the other thigh. Don't forget the head needs support.

Step 3. Gently rub and pat the baby's back. If this does not work, repeat, but with a little more force.

Sitting

Step 1. Place the cloth in your lap.

Step 2. Place the baby in a sitting position on your lap, leaning forward a little.

Step 3. Support the baby's chest and chin with one hand.

Step 4. Gently rub and pat the baby's back. If this does not work, repeat, but with a little more force.

10

How to Change a Diaper

OK, I realize that this isn't the fun part, but it's got to be done, and Mommy isn't going to be around every time to do it. So, if you want the kid to stop screaming, listen up.

What You Will Need

1. A baby with a dirty diaper.
2. A soft towel you don't mind possibly getting doo-doo and wee-wee on.
3. A changing table or counter space.
4. A clean diaper.
5. A washcloth or diaper wipes.
6. Baby powder.
7. A place to put a soiled diaper. I do *not* recommend putting it in the kitchen garbage can.
8. A clothespin for your nose.

Tips

1. Don't ever leave or take your attention from the baby. *Always* have one hand on the baby.
2. If you are changing a boy, place the clean diaper over his penis. It is not uncommon for a boy to start whizzing all over the place. This will prevent him from whizzing all over you.

Step 1. Place a towel over a counter or baby-changing table.

Step 2. Place the baby on his back and remove the dirty diaper. Look at how it is attached, to help you when you are putting the new diaper on.

Step 3. Hold the baby by the ankles and carefully lift the baby's hips. You don't have to lift him off the table by the feet, just enough to slide the diaper out.

Step 4. Remove the diaper, *folding the soiled part in.*

Step 5. With a warm, *not hot*, washcloth, clean the baby off. *Wipe the girls from front to back and boys from back to front.*

Step 6. After the baby is clean, pat him or her dry. (Don't continue to wipe; this can irritate the baby's skin.)

Step 7. Put baby powder in the new diaper, just a sprinkle—it doesn't need to be caked in there. The powder keeps the baby from sticking to the diaper. It's the same reasoning behind why flour is placed in gum wrappers; it keeps the gum from sticking.

Step 8. Put the clean diaper under the baby. If it is a disposable diaper, make sure that it is facing the right way. It doesn't matter with cloth diapers.

Step 9. Bring the bottom part of the diaper up through the baby's legs. If it is a boy, aim his penis down. If you don't, he could end up peeing all over his shirt the next time.

Step 10. Secure the back edge of the diaper *over the front* part of the diaper with adhesive tabs. (Usually attached to disposables.) Make sure you don't stick the tape to the baby's skin. If you are using cloth diapers, make sure you don't stick the baby with the safety pins. It is good to place your hand in between the baby's skin and the cloth you are pinning. That way you can prick yourself and not the baby.

Tips

1. The diaper should be tight enough to avoid leaking, but not too tight. If it is too tight it will irritate the baby's skin. Use your common sense again.
2. If you are not at home, put the used diaper in a plastic bag for disposal.

11

How to Tie a Tie

When I was doing research for this book, I was amazed to find that there were several ways of tying a tie. However, for a few reasons I decided to explain only how to tie the standard necktie and the double windsor. First, tying a tie is hard enough without having to choose which knot you want; second, if you learn these two ways of tying a tie it should be one more way than you really need to know; third, it was less work for me.

General Tie Rules and Measuring Tips

One of the hardest things to get right when tying a tie is the length. Fortunately, there are a few rules you can follow.

1. When you are done, the tie should not hang lower than the top of your belt buckle. Guys with ties that are too short are perceived as geeks, and guys with ties that are too long are thought of as snakes.
2. Never let the narrow end of the tie hang lower than the wide end.
3. When you begin, the wide end of the tie should be on the side of your dominant hand. If you are right-handed, the wide end of the tie should be on your right side.
4. To measure a tie properly you can do one of two things. First, measure your tie out so the narrow end is at the fourth button down on your shirt. (The collar button is one, then count down three more.) The second way to measure is to let the broad end of the tie hang down twice as long as the narrow end. To check this, fold the broad end up to your neck. The narrow side of the tie should be equal to the folded wide side.

The Standard Neck Tie

Step 1. Take the narrow side of your tie in your nondominant hand about three inches down from your neck.

Step 2. Take the broad end of the tie and pass it across and over this spot. Hold it at that spot.

Step 3. Take the broad end around behind that spot, and around the back of the narrow end. Wrap it over again like in step 2.

Step 4. Put the broad end behind the spot where you are holding it and put it up through the **V** in the tie. (The **V** is the area between the collar and the spot where you are holding it.)

Step 5. Bring the broad end of the tie through the **V** and let it fold over and hang down. Now grab the tie by the tip of the broad end and tuck it between the top wrap of the tie and the spot you have been holding.

Step 6. Firmly pull the knot up toward your neck. Look in the mirror and make sure it is straight and even. If it is not, try to adjust it by pulling the knot and the narrow end. As you will come to find, tying a tie is an art, and even the best of us have to sometimes try several times before we get it right.

The Double Windsor

The double windsor is bigger than the standard necktie knot. It is favored by politicians, businessmen, and people who think they are hot shit. So, if you have a political rally to attend, or want to be a cool guy at your next meeting, then this is for you. Actually, it is a cool knot, and if worn with the right suit it will help you get laid. Women love a stylish guy.

Since the double windsor is a bigger knot, you are going to need more length on the broad side. Instead of counting down four buttons, count down three. If you don't know what I am talking about then read the tie-tying tips section.

Step 1. Grab the narrow side of the tie with your nondominant hand about 2 inches down from your neck. Take the broad side and pass over and across that spot. Hold it there with your nondominant hand.

Step 2. Pass the broad side behind and out in front. Then down through the top of the **Y** and *back* out the *same* side. This is very awkward, but just do it. The tie will be backward with the label facing you. Don't worry, you are doing it right.

Step 3. Wrap the broad side across the front, then behind again, and *up* through the **Y**. Then let the broad end hang down.

Step 4. Take the broad end hanging down and tuck it between the *last* wrap and the spot you have been holding. (It looks weird, but trust me.)

Step 5. Gently pull the broad side of the tie down and the knot together. In this step you are pulling the knot together as well as sliding it up toward the collar. Use one hand to pull on the broad end of the tie and the other to work the knot into its proper shape. (It will now look like a wide funnel.) Make sure the smaller wrap of the knot doesn't slip down the smaller side, and make sure it stays in the outer wrap. As the knot moves up and tightens, grab the narrow end of the tie and gently pull. This will further tighten the knot.

You know that you have done it right if there is a dimple just below the end of the knot. Also make sure the tie is straight and the proper length. And now, congratulations are in order, because getting this right is a bitch.

12

How to Tie a Bow Tie

I only have two tips for you. Have fun, and make sure you have plenty of time. Some bow ties have a clip in back that allows you to adjust the length until it's just right for you. Make sure it is the right length. Bow ties are narrow in the middle and have an hourglass shape at both ends. The narrow part is where the knot will be tied. The wider part forms the loops.

Step 1. This is going to be confusing, and could take a while, so I will keep it simple. Put the bow tie around your buttoned shirt collar, and let the side of your tie that corresponds with your dominant hand hang down about two inches longer than the other. If you write with your left hand the bow tie will hang down two inches more on your left side than on your right side.

Step 2. Hold the tie just above the widening point with your nondominant hand. This is where you will tie the knot.

Step 3. Take the *longer* end and cross it *over* this spot. Put it behind and out through the top. Let it hang down. This knot is permanent and can be pulled tight. Make sure the end on top is still a little longer.

Step 4. Take the shorter end and fold it over on top of itself, *not* behind it. The narrow part should be right on top of the actual knot and the wide part becomes the edge of the loop. Hold this loop at the base with your nondominant hand.

Step 5. Using your dominant hand, wrap the longer end over and down, then around *behind* the first loop. Make sure you don't twist the tie, but wrap it carefully around.

Step 6. Insert the longer end through the knot. In this step, push the loop with your finger *through* the central knot. Pull it through. You are now creating the second loop.

Step 7. Hold the first loop and pull the new loop tighter. *Make sure you don't pull the ends out.* Pull evenly and adjust the final shape.

That's it. However, all bow ties will have to be played with to get the ends straight and the knot square. Make sure the tie is not too tight or it will ride up on the shirt, and you will also pass out. (You will never be able to recover from the mental anguish caused by passing out because your bow tie is too tight.) On the other hand, a loose tie makes you look like a slob. Basically, what this means is that if you are going to take the time to tie this type of tie, then do it right. Finally, in case you were wondering, the tabs stay *behind* the bow. Don't forget that!

13

How to Hook Up a Stereo

Stereos are similar to VCRs in the sense that once you get the feel for how the setup procedure is supposed to flow, you realize that it is really easy. Every stereo is different, but they all work in a pretty similar fashion. For example, the best way to describe how to set up different stereos is to compare the process to driving a car. Every car is different, but once you know how to drive one car you can pretty much drive them all. The same thing goes for stereos.

The Components

As technology has become more advanced, so has the difficulty level for setting up a stereo. It is not just tape decks and record players anymore, but everything from TVs to personal computers. Although the complexity of stereos has changed, they still have the same basic components.

Basic Components

1. Tuner
2. Tape deck(s)
3. CD player
4. Speakers

Optional Components

1. Turntable (Once standard, now optional.)
2. TV
3. Additional speakers
4. DAT player
5. DVD player
6. Personal computer (I have only seen this once, but it was really cool.)

The Mother Ship and Her Attachments

The one most important thing to remember about setting up a stereo is that the tuner is the power source, and is also what the other accessories (tape deck, CD player) are plugged in to. After you have figured out where you are going to put your stereo, it is time to hook it up.

The CD Player

To attach the CD player to the tuner you will need a stereo cable. A stereo cable is actually two cables that are joined together and have plugs on both ends. On the back of the CD player you will find two jack sockets, usually labeled ("left" and "right"), and color coded (either red and black or red and white). Take one side of the cable and plug it into the corresponding jack. For example, plug the red cable that is labeled "right" into the jack that is colored red and labeled "right." Next look on the back of the tuner and there will be similar jacks that will be labeled "CD player." Plug the corresponding plugs into the jacks located on the back of the tuner. Also, in many cases, you will find a regular electrical outlet or a number of outlets on the back of the tuner. The purpose of this is so you can plug your CD player and tape deck into the actual tuner, allowing you to turn off your stereo system. You only have to turn the power off on the tuner, and not turn each component off individually—which also saves wall outlet space.

The Tape Deck

Setting up the tape deck, and any other components you may have, is almost exactly the same as setting up the CD player. The difference is that instead of having to hook up only two connections you have to hook up four. There is a stereo wire for both the "play" section and the "record" section. Remember, plug the corresponding plugs into the jacks located on the back of the tape deck, then to the tuner. Follow basically the same directions for any other components you will be connecting to the tuner.

The Speakers

The speakers are the most important part of your stereo. You can have a great CD player, but if your speakers suck then who cares about the CD player? The wire that connects the speakers to the tuner is actually two wires connected in the middle. Using a wire cutter, separate the speaker wires from each other for about 2–3 inches at each end. Next, using a wire stripper, strip the rubber coating from the last half inch of each wire. For two speakers you will have two wires with two exposed wires on each end. One side of the speaker wire should be marked (usually with a stripe), and the other side is plain. Insert the marked side of the speaker wire into the red "+" connection on the terminal in the back of the speaker. Next, insert the unmarked side of the wire into the black "–" connection. Lock down both wires. After you have attached the wires to your speakers, take a look at the back of your tuner. If your tuner has surround-sound capabilities, there may be connections for four or five sets of speakers. You will only be using the connections that are labeled either "Front" or "A." Insert the wires from the speakers to the corresponding connection on the tuner. The red "+" wire is inserted into the red "+" connection. Repeat for the other speaker or speakers.

Tips

1. Remember the tuner is the power source, and the other components are plugged in to it.
2. If you have purchased a complicated component system, read the directions thoroughly.
3. If you are stacking your stereo components, don't place anything (like a towel) in between each section. There are vents on each component that need to be open so each part can get proper ventilation. If the vents are blocked, the stereo can short out. Put your tuner on top of the other components since it will need the most ventilation.

4. The speakers should be at least 6 feet apart.
5. Don't plan to put speakers behind couches or drapes; the sound will be severely muffled.

14

How to Set Up a VCR

I remember one day in the late fall of 1977 when I got a call from a close friend. His father had come home late the night before from a trip overseas and had brought with him a brand-new Sony videocassette recorder. Even though I didn't know what a videocassette recorder was at the time, I knew that if it was a Sony, it had to be good. I promptly rode my bike to my friend's house. The VCR was a table-top model that weighed about 50 pounds, and was about 2½ feet long, 1½ feet wide, and 1 foot thick. The cassette tapes loaded into a door that popped opened from the top, and from what I remember it seemed to have about 2,000 different knobs, switches, and buttons. My friend and I were studying the new gadget when his father entered the room and scolded us because the VCR was, as he explained, "not a toy." He said that it had cost him $1,200 and he had to pay extra to get the simulated wood-grain finish so it would match the coffee table. A day or so later, I asked my friend's father if he had any movies we could watch. With that question, my friend's dad sort of smiled and said, "Well, I have a few movies I can watch, but nothing that would interest you." Little did he know that I would get another phone call from my friend a few weeks later and he would ask me if I wanted to watch a movie about the Dallas Cowboys starring some girl named Debbie.

The Problem With VCRs

On the back of VCRs, among the numerous other plugs and switches, there are two coaxial cable ports that are usually labeled "In" and "Out." The reason people have problems hooking up VCRs is that these port labels are misleading. In almost all scenarios where a VCR is improperly hooked up, the person who did the hookup thought that the cable that goes from the VCR to the TV should be plugged into the "In" port. Even if you *do* understand how to connect a TV and VCR, like myself, it is easy to understand why a person may get confused and think that the cable is plugged "In." "Where does the cable go? I don't know, plug it 'In' here." Imagine if you had to hook up a home computer and all of the plugs were labeled "In" or "Out" or "It goes here" or "Try this one"? The electronics industry needs to realize that not everyone is a rocket scientist and adopt a better VCR labeling system.

The best way to understand how to hook up a VCR is to look at this procedure from a different point of view. Don't think about the fact that the ports are labeled as "In" and "Out," but rather look at the VCR's assembly as if it were a flow chart. If you are watching a movie, remember that it comes "out" of the VCR and "in" to the TV. Did a light switch just come on in your head?

Different Ways to Hook Up a VCR

There are actually a number of ways to hook up a TV and VCR. You can hook up cable TV to your VCR, you can hook up two TVs to your VCR, you can hook up two VCRs to each other so you can record movies, and I am not going to even get into hooking up a satellite dish. Instead of confusing you with too much information, I am going to explain the two most common ways: a simple TV and VCR hookup, and a TV and VCR hookup with cable TV.

Simple TV and VCR Hookup

Remember the flow chart. If you are attaching a borrowed VCR to your TV and are only going to watch a few movies, then return it to its owner, all you have to remember is that the coaxial cable goes *from the "Out" port on the VCR to the back of the TV.* Then make sure the TV is turned to the proper channel (usually 3 or 4), push play, and sit back and relax. Wasn't that simple?

Hooking Up a TV, VCR, and Cable TV

Connecting a TV and VCR with cable TV is a little more complicated than just hooking up a TV and VCR, but if you remember to think of it in terms of a flow chart, you will find it pretty easy.

Connecting Your TV, VCR, and Cable Through a Separate Cable Box

Most modern VCRs also act as cable boxes that allow you to hook your cable directly from the wall socket into the VCR and then to the TV— basically eliminating the need for a cable box and another remote. However, some VCRs may only allow you to get certain channels, or they may be needed to view pay-per-view channels. If this is the case, don't worry, once you get the grasp of how everything works it is easy. Just like riding a bike.

Step 1. Attach a cable that runs from the wall outlet to the cable box. Attach that cable to the plug that says "In" or "Cable In."

Step 2. Attach another cable to the other plug on the cable box that says "Out" or "Cable Out" to the plug on the VCR that says "In."

Step 3. Attach a cable to the VCR's other coaxial cable plug that says "Out" and plug it in to the TV.

Connecting Your TV, VCR, and Cable *Without* a Separate Cable Box

Basically all you are doing is removing the cable box and hooking the cable directly to the VCR.

Step 1. Attach a cable that runs from the cable outlet on the wall to the plug on the VCR that says "In."

Step 2. Attach another cable that runs from the "Out" plug on the VCR to the TV. Now your VCR is acting as a cable box, and you should be able to change channels with your VCR remote.

Tips and Terms

1. Coaxial cable is a ⅛-inch-thick wire that ends with a plug that resembles a needle. That very small wire has to be inserted into a hole in the plug's receptacle. The wire (usually white or black in color) is then screwed into place.
2. To view most VCRs the TV must be tuned in to channel 3 or 4. There is usually a switch on the back of the VCR that allows you to choose. Make sure this switch is set properly before you try to play a videotape.
3. Make sure you clean your VCR's heads about every 3–6 months with a cleaning tape. The heads basically translate the information on the tape and allow it to be viewed on the TV screen. Dirty heads equal a fuzzy movie.
4. Make sure the coaxial cable is screwed on tight. A loose wire can also be the cause of a fuzzy picture.

PART TWO

Tying One On—An Apron, That Is: A Crash Course in Cooking

15

How to Separate an Egg

You should know how to separate an egg because egg whites are included in the recipe for making a good Margarita or Ramos Fizz. They also make good omelets.

What You Will Need

1. An egg
2. A bowl
3. A sink

Version 1. My Way

The easiest, but messiest, way to separate an egg is to do it with your hands. This is not for the squeamish.

Step 1. Wash your hands (as if a raw egg in a Margarita weren't enough) and place the bowl next to the sink.

Step 2. Hold your nondominant hand over the bowl. Crack the egg, and empty the contents into your hand. While keeping the yolk in the palm of your hand, let the egg white run through your fingers and into the bowl. This is actually easier than it sounds, but it is very messy. You can either throw the egg yolk down the sink drain, or feel free to use it in a recipe, such as hollandaise sauce, custard, egg-sauce salad dressing, etc.

Version 2. The Non-Messy Way

I recommend using this method only when someone else is watching you separate the egg. If you are cooking or concocting something for that person, they might not appreciate the fact that you are putting the egg in your hand. Some people couldn't care less, but others will be very offended. (I don't recommend hanging out with those people anyway.)

Step 1. Wash your hands!

Step 2. Carefully crack the egg on the side of the bowl and instead of emptying the contents into the bowl, turn the egg on end, and pull off the top, letting most of the egg white fall into the bowl (don't throw the top shell away just yet). Once you have the egg shell separated, pour the contents of the bottom part of the egg, (it contains the remaining egg white and the egg yolk) back and forth between the top and bottom part of the shell, as you are doing this let the egg white drop into the bowl, and try to keep the yolk in the egg shell. Be careful not to let the yolk sac touch the sharp edges of the cracked shell, otherwise you will have scrambled eggs.

This technique of egg separation is very difficult and will take practice to learn. The first few times you will either break the yolk or it will accidentally get poured into the bowl with the egg white. For those reasons I recommend version number 1, it will save you time, and nine times out of ten you will make a mess anyway.

16

How to Select a Melon

How to Select a Melon is included in this book for two reasons. The first is that if you happen to like honeydew or cantaloupe then you can learn how to pick the ripest one. The second reason is to impress women. Not just to impress women whom you want to date, but also mothers and grandmothers. Used properly, this is one of those skills that can be an integral part to get that first date and also give an excellent first impression. For example, if you are in the grocery store and there is a hot babe trying to pick out a cantaloupe, then you will have a reason to talk to her. This approach is much more effective than stalking her for an hour up and down each aisle—trust me on this.

Step 1. How Does It Look?

The first way to determine the ripeness of a melon is by looking at it. A honeydew melon is *not* ripe if its skin is any shade of green and it has prominent green veins running through it. A ripe honeydew will be a pale yellow color, and the veins running through it will be a lighter yellow. Cantaloupe are similar in this respect. Their skin will be pale (not brown) and the veins will be orange or orange yellow. Cantaloupes are not ripe if the veins are green. Another distinguishing feature of melons is a flat, discolored spot on one of the sides. This mark means that the melon has ripened on the vine and that it has flattened under its own weight, and the color is lost because the melon sat shaded in the soil.

Step 2. How Does It Feel?

Both a ripe cantaloupe and a honeydew should feel firm but not rock hard. It will give a little if you lightly squeeze it, but it should not feel like a sponge. If it is too soft, it has gone bad. The stem end of the melon is the best place to press. (The stem end is where the fruit was attached to the vine. It will be slightly flatter than the rounded flower end and have a round stem mark in the top center.)

Step 3. How Does It Sound?

If you are a beginner at picking a ripe melon, then using sound may not be a good indicator for you to use initially. However, the more melons you pick, the more experience you will have, and before you know it, all you will have to do is to give a honeydew a good thump to pick a ripe one.

Here is what you have to do to pick a honeydew or cantaloupe by using your ear. As if you were going to knock on someone's door, give the melon a few good thumps. A ripe melon should have a deep, thick sound. An unripe melon will have a higher pitch, and will sound hollow. Also, as a honeydew melon ripens, the seeds in the core become detached from the part of the fruit that holds them in place. As a result, a ripe honeydew will rattle if it is shaken. A cantaloupe does share this characteristic, but sometimes the seeds will not come loose and it may not always rattle when shaken.

Step 4. How Does It Smell?

If you have a good sense of smell, give a sniff or two to the stem end of the fruit. The stronger and more delicious the smell, the riper and sweeter the fruit.

17

How to Open a Coconut

I like coconut. I like coconut cake, I like coconut candy, I like raw coconut, and I especially like coconut pie, but when I was doing research for this book I started to look at coconut a little differently. The reason for this is because coconut (the actual white stuff) is called "meat." That's right, coconut is considered meat. Now, when I think of meat I think of steak or chicken, not coconut. It is as if someone told me that there is a species of fish that lives off the coast of Aruba that is called chocolate candy. It's not candy, it's fish. It's not meat, it's coconut! I don't know but it just doesn't sit right with me.

There are actually a few different types of coconut, but the coconut I am referring to is the same one you are thinking about, the one you can find in your local supermarket. It is brown, hairy, and about the size of a softball. You can tell if a coconut is ripe if it doesn't have any cracks in the outer shell, and when you shake it, it sounds like it is full of liquid. (That is because it is.)

What You Will Need

1. A hammer or mallet
2. A regular screwdriver or ice pick
3. A knife
4. A container to hold the coconut milk.

Step 1. Draining the Liquid

Locate the three dark eyes on the smaller end of the coconut. Clean your screwdriver or ice pick and then place it on one of these eyes. Using your hammer, tap the screwdriver into the coconut. After you have broken through the shell (you can tell when you can move the screwdriver in and out of the coconut easily), pull the screwdriver out and empty the coconut milk into a container. The milk can be used in recipes (like a Piña Colada), or it can be drunk by itself.

Step 2. Finding the Breaking Point

It is a lot easier to open a coconut than you might think. There is a natural stress point where the coconut's outer shell cracks open. Your job is to speed up this natural process. Put the coconut on a flat surface, like a counter. Locate an area about two to three inches down from the smaller end (the end where the "eyes" are located. Coconuts are shaped like eggs; the ends are of different sizes).

Step 3. Cracking the Shell

Take the screwdriver by the shaft, not by the handle, and tap with some force on that spot. After a few taps, rotate the coconut, and tap the same distance down from the smaller end. Keep tapping, and rotating, until a small crack in the outer shell appears.

Step 4. Breaking Open the Coconut

When a crack in the shell appears, take the screwdriver, insert the point, tap it with the hammer, and pry open the coconut. After a little force the coconut should split completely open. Use a knife to cut out the white coconut meat.

Tips

1. Make sure your screwdriver is clean.
2. Don't use a knife in place of the screwdriver; it can easily slip and cut you.
3. You may have to use some force when tapping on the screwdriver. Coconuts have a very hard shell.
4. It is also possible to whack open the coconut with a hammer, but that will make a huge mess.

18

How to Grill the Perfect Steak

Cooking the perfect steak is an art that takes years of grilling experience to master—*not!* I was first taught how to cook a steak when I was working in a restaurant for a summer as a dishwasher. It was an OK job. The pay sucked, but the waitresses were hot, and since I was fifteen years old, that was a huge benefit. One of the cool things about the job was that when it was a little slow I got to help the cook. I didn't realize it until later that she was just lazy and didn't want to do her job, but at the time I thought she was being nice. The cook was in her forties, a total slob, big as a house, dirty; she smoked, had bad breath, and sometimes I couldn't tell if she was chopping onions or just had b.o. However, she knew her way around a kitchen.

On one particularly busy day when her grill cook, some Mexican guy who was high all the time, didn't show up, she pulled me out of the sink and into the kitchen to help out. I felt like a field goal kicker at the Superbowl with ten seconds to go in the fourth quarter. It was either kick a 55-yard field goal or lose the game. Tensions were high. She needed someone to cook the five New York strip steaks that had just been ordered, or to at least watch them burn, and she chose *me*. I was put in charge of a hundred dollars of prime beef, and I was being asked to cook them for some well-paying customers.

I felt so screwed; I had only cooked a hamburger about three times before. I knew I was going to mess up. The cook soon realized how clueless I was. She grabbed me by the shoulders and calmly said, "Do you know how to cook a steak?" Like a three-year-old child who had just written all over his daddy's freshly painted walls with crayons, I softly, and sheep-ishly said no. I thought she was going to go crazy, but to my surprise she calmly said, "Well, then, I will teach you."

As the night went on, I cooked more steaks, and to my, and everyone else's, surprise, none of the steaks was sent back. One guy even told the waitress that it was the best steak he had ever had! I got very lucky that night, and even though I did a good job, I don't recommend the same crash course in steak grilling for everyone. What I am going to tell you is exactly what the cook taught me that night.

Touch Technique

You prod the steak with your finger to determine how done it is. To some this may sound gross, and I'm sure you don't want anyone touching your food. However, it is the best way to determine how a steak is cooked, and trust me, it is not going to kill you.

Rare. Let your dominant hand hang limp. Using the index finger of your other hand touch the muscle right above the web between your thumb and index finger. That's how a rare steak feels.

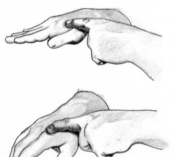

Medium. Close the space between your thumb and index finger. You don't have to use a lot of force, just hold it closed. Touch the same place on your hand you would touch to check for a rare steak. That's how a medium steak feels.

Well. Touch *right behind* the knuckle of the index finger of your dominant hand. This should be the same consistency as a well-done steak.

Thermometer Technique

If you are totally opposed to the touching technique, you can use a meat thermometer.

Rare. 140 Degrees

Medium. 160 Degrees

Well. 180 Degrees

Always take the steak off the grill 10 degrees lower than you want and cover it up with tin foil, as it will continue to cook. For example, if you're cooking a medium steak take it off the grill when the thermometer reads 150 degrees.

Tips

1. If you are going to use a meat thermometer, I suggest that you leave it in the meat the whole time it's cooking. If you just stick the thermometer in the steak every so often you will not get an accurate reading.
2. Always let meat stand a few minutes before you cut it. Steaks will continue to cook slightly when taken off the grill. This cool-down time allows it to stop cooking, and the juices to settle.

19

How to Carve a Turkey

Women do not carve turkeys; this is men's work. Sure as shootin' you will be asked sometime in your life by some woman, whether it is your grandmother, mother, wife, or girlfriend, to carve a turkey (and this applies to smaller fowl, too). Don't screw up! Your manhood is at stake here.

Actually, it's not that hard to do, but it should be done with some élan (that means "class" for all you non-French speakers out there). The best way to slice meat is to use a meat slicer (makes sense, doesn't it?). A meat slicer is a long, *serrated* knife with a blade about an inch wide and nine or ten inches long. It has a rounded, not pointed, end, and the blade is an even width and not tapered. The serrated edge on the knife allows for an even cut, while a straight edge, such as that on a chef's knife, can, and often will, go willy-nilly on you.

If you don't have a meat slicer, then use a bread slicer. A bread slicer is a knife with a blade similar to a meat slicer, except it has a thinner blade (about one-half inch). If you have to, use two knives to carve the bird. Use a chef's knife or some other large, strong knife to cut the joints and then use the bread slicer to slice the breast and thigh meat.

After you have sliced the meat, pick it up between the fork and the tip of the knife (not with your fingers; this is what I mean when I say "class") and put it on the serving platter. If you are too spastic to accomplish this, spear the meat with the fork and then push it off the fork with the flat blade of the knife onto the serving dish. The following steps will help explain the carving process further.

What You Will Need

1. A sharp carving knife
2. A large carving fork
3. A cutting board or platter
4. A dishtowel
5. A cooked turkey

Tips

1. This can be a messy job, so be prepared.
2. Expect to have trouble cutting the legs and wings away from the body at the joint. It's OK, everyone does, just try not to butcher it too badly. The trick is to find the place where the two bones join and cut through it. If you hit bone, back off and try again.
3. Not all of your cuts will be uniform. Don't expect your slices to look perfect as they do in a TV dinner.
4. Relax. Carving is in a man's genes.
5. Use a sharp knife.

Step 1. Preparing Your Work Space

- First make sure you have a spacious area to carve your turkey. Carving can be awkward and cumbersome.
- Next, place the dishtowel under the cutting board or platter. The towel keeps the cutting board from slipping and sliding on the counter.
- Let your bird cool for about 10–15 minutes after being removed from the oven.
- Wash your hands!

Step 2. Removing Legs and Wings

- The first thing to remember is that you carve one side of the bird at a time. Take off the leg and wing on one side, then carve the breast on that side. When you are done removing all the meat on one side, start on the other.

- After picking a side to start, grab the end of the drumstick and pull it outward from the bird. (Don't yank it, you just need to pull hard enough to get to the joint.) Take the knife and force it into the joint of the leg and body. Sometimes it will separate easily, but if not, you may have to cut through the joint. Feel for the connecting point between the two bones and sever the two bones from each other. Don't try to saw through the bone itself.

- You can either leave the drumstick and thigh attached, or separate them. To separate the drumstick and thigh, use a sharp knife to cut the joint. To cut the meat off the bone, hold the unseparated leg up by the drumstick on the carving board and begin to slice the meat off the thigh. Always cut toward the carving board. Move on to the drumstick and work your way around the leg.

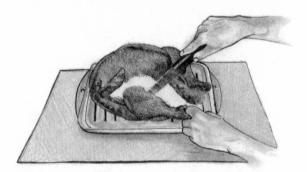

- To separate the wing from the body, you can either pull the wing away from the body with your fingers (just like you did with the leg), or you can use the fork to pry it away. Either way, insert the knife and cut the wing away from the body separating it at the joint.

Step 3. Carving the Breast

- Remove the skin and use the fork to balance the turkey. When you begin to cut a turkey breast, place the knife parallel to the bird, then turn the knife inward about 15 degrees. This should put the knife at the plumpest part of the breast.
- First cut about a 2-inch-wide slice from the plumpest area of the breast, halfway down.
- Continue to slice downward, and allow the pieces to become larger as you cut higher and higher on the breast.

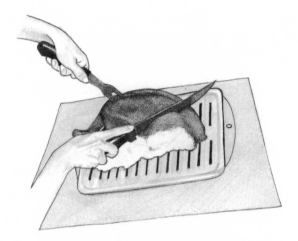

- As you get closer to the rib cage the pieces may become different shapes and sizes. Don't worry about this, it is natural. Between the spine and the rib cage is a chunk of white meat about an inch or two wide; don't try to slice it all the way down the rib cage. Just slice from the top of the bird to the top of the rib cage.

Step 4. Carve the Other Side

Turn the bird around and carve the other side, starting from step 2.

20

How to Shuck an Oyster

Oysters are tasty little critters that live on the seabed in shallow coastal waters. The shell consists of two valves, a left and right (or top and bottom,

depending on your view) valve, one of which is flatter and the other a bit rounder or cup shaped. The valves are joined at the tapered end of the mollusk by a flexible hinge-like ligament that opens the oyster. An adductor muscle is attached to the middle of both valves; it strongly clamps the shell shut. When the adductor is relaxed, the elastic ligament works in the opposite direction and opens the valves. Your mission, if you choose to accept it, requires that you cut both the ligament and the adductor muscle to gain the delicious prize inside.

Oysters are best from September to April (the old "any month with an 'R' in it" rule of thumb). Oysters spawn from May through August and are not as meaty or tasty during these months due to the fact that they are expending their energy getting laid. They are, however, edible during the summer months but are not quite as sweet or plump.

Some people feel that the warm summer months bring more bacteria to the shellfish and that's why you shouldn't eat them at that time of year. There is little evidence for this since most oysters are bred on oyster farms, but if you still don't feel right about it, then don't eat them raw—cook them. Cooking kills any harmful bacteria and there are myriad ways to prepare oysters, including barbecuing, steaming, poaching, stewing, etc. Don't eat oysters that you or someone else has clawed up from the pond; 99 percent of shellfish poisoning cases result from uninspected and noncertified shellfish.

What You Will Need

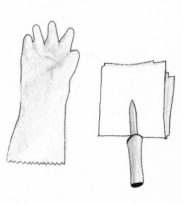

1. Fresh oysters
2. An oyster knife (a butter knife or screwdriver will do in a pinch, but it is *not* recommended)
3. A bar towel
4. A filled sink or bucket of water
5. Heavy duty work or rubber gloves
6. Ice

Picking a Fresh Oyster

The key to picking fresh oysters is to make sure that you buy them from a reputable fish store; also make sure they are closed tight. When oysters are in standing water, they open slightly to allow water with nutrients into their shells. If they stay open when they are handled, they are past their prime and may be bad. Test them by squeezing the shell together between your thumb and forefinger. If the shell closes immediately when you do this, they are OK to eat. Do not buy oysters with cracked or broken shells.

Store your oysters on ice or on a tray in a refrigerator at between 34 and 40 degrees, *cup side down,* covered by a damp cloth until they are ready to serve. They will keep fresh for a day this way. *Never* store them in fresh water or in an airtight container (this will kill them). Make sure your oysters always have plenty of ice, and occasionally check them to make sure none have spoiled. Sometimes you have to open them to know if they have spoiled. If the meat inside is dry, has an off odor (oysters should smell like seawater), or is pink, discard the oyster.

Step 1. Shucking oysters can be a messy job. Make sure you have a well-covered and easily cleanable work station. Doing this outdoors, if possible, is best.

Step 2. Oyster shells can be *extremely* sharp. To avoid cutting your hand, put a heavy-duty glove at this time on your nondominant hand. Grab an oyster with your dominant hand and wash it off in your bucket of water or filled sink.

Step 3. Take the bar towel, fold it in half, then fold it in half again. Put it in your nondominant hand. (Right-handed people put the folded towel in your left hand.) The reason I prefer a towel *and* a glove is because it is possible when trying to pop the hinge of the oyster to slip and jam the knife into your hand. Folded towels offer a lot more protection than a heavy duty glove alone. The knife will go right through the one-layer glove as opposed to the four-layer towel.

Step 4. Look for the hinge of the oyster shell. It will be located at the smaller end of the oyster where the two shell valves meet. You should find a distinct seam. Think of this seam as a lock and your oyster knife as the key.

Step 5. Hold the oyster cup side down with the narrow end in your palm. Insert and *twist* the knife into the seam. Do not use excessive force, but firmly work the knife back and forth until the oyster pops open. This is a matter of finesse rather than strength. Once the seam has been broken, gradually twist and insert the knife around the oyster until you have almost separated the two halves. Try to remember to keep the oyster parallel to the ground. This keeps the oyster level and prevents you from spilling the oyster juice everywhere.

Step 6. Making sure to keep the oyster level, slide the knife between the shell and the actual oyster and scrape it back and forth. This step cuts the oyster's adductor

muscle. You will know when the muscle is cut because you can separate the two halves. Discard the flat top shell. Place the bottom valve on a bed of ice or shuck it into a bowl with its liquor to cook it later.

Condiments

You can satisfy the condiment requirements of 99 percent of oyster eaters by supplying the following items: Saltine crackers, lemon wedges, Tabasco sauce, cocktail sauce, and horseradish. The other 1 percent like to eat their oysters condiment free.

Cocktail Sauce

¼ cup ketchup
¼ cup chili sauce
Juice of ½ lemon
2 tablespoons of Worcestershire sauce
Horseradish to taste

For a less-sweet, more-zesty sauce, omit the ketchup and mix the chili sauce and horseradish in equal amounts. Add Tabasco sauce to taste.

21

How to Eat King Crab Legs

The best way to describe how delicious King crab legs are is with this example. One night I went out to dinner with one of my friends, Mike, and his four-year-old son Connor. We went up the street to a local diner to grab a sandwich. Connor and I had a conversation.

> ME: "What are you going to order for dinner tonight, Connor?"
> CONNOR: "I want crab legs."
> ME: *After a long pause so I could look over the menu* "Connor, I don't think crab legs are on the menu."
> CONNOR: "But crab legs are yummy."

After Connor had made his dinner request, to tell you the truth, it made both Mike and I want crab legs too. We decided to go up the street to a local seafood restaurant to have crab legs for dinner because Connor had hit the nail on the head. Crab legs are yummy.

King crab legs can be bought at most fish markets. Unless you live in Alaska, I doubt that you'll find any live ones at your fish market. They will come already cooked. Ask your local fishmonger which method he recommends to warm them up.

What You Will Need

1. Newspaper—make sure you cover the area where you will be eating crab legs, it can get very messy and this makes for an easier clean up.
2. A Medium Sized Knife—A steak knife will do.
3. A Mallet or Nutcracker
4. Paper Towels
5. Melted Butter—You cannot enjoy crab legs without hot melted butter.

Step 1. The Crab Leg

After you have selected a cluster of crab legs, break off one of the legs from where it attaches to the body. Next, take a good look at the leg. You will see that there are four distinct sections. The biggest section is the upper thigh. It is about 2–3 inches long and contains the biggest and best-tasting pieces of meat. The next two sections make up the lower part of the leg. The first part of the lower leg is about an inch long, while the second part is about two to three times that size. These parts also contain good tasting crab meat but they are smaller than the piece you will find in the upper leg. The final section of the crab leg resembles a toe or foot. It is about an inch long, and it contains no meat.

Step 2. Where to Start?

The best place to start when eating a King crab leg is with the final section, the piece that contains no meat. The reason that this is the best place to start is because there is a tendon that runs about half-way up the length of the leg. It is best to pull the tendon out before you try to remove the crab meat, because once the tendon has been removed the crab meat is easier to remove from the shell. Snap off the last section, and pull out the tendon and discard.

Step 3. Getting to the Crab Meat

Once the tendon has been removed, break apart the crab leg at the joints, separating it into three pieces. Since the best meat is in the largest section of the leg, this is a good place to start. Grab the upper part of the crab leg between your *thumbs and forefingers*. Next, try to break only the side of the shell that is facing *away from you*, don't break the shell *all the way through*, just try to crack it. Once you have cracked that side of the shell, turn it over, and using the same grip as before, crack the other side of the shell. By breaking the sides of the crab shell one at a time, and not all the way through, you will be able to remove the shell without damaging the crab meat. The reason you don't want to break the shell completely in half, is because if you break all the way through the shell then you will also break through the crab meat. Instead of having one large piece of crab meat that can be easily removed from the shell, you will have to dig out the crab meat from the shell with a fork. This can be a mess and a pain in the ass. Follow the same technique with the other two sections of the crab leg.

Removing Meat From the Claws

The claw and the claw arm are extremely tough to break. As a result, most people try to use a nutcracker or hammer to try to break through the shell. I personally do not recommend this method, because nine times out of ten, you end up damaging the crab meat itself. I don't know about you, but I can't stand shell in my crab. It is best to use a knife and a mallet.

Step 1. Put the claw on the table with the inside of the pincers facing up. Take your knife and place it slightly behind where the pincers meet. Then take your mallet and tap on the knife. What you want to do is to cut the claw about half-way through, not to cut it into two pieces.

Step 2. After you have put a cut in the claw, pick up the claw in both hands and carefully snap it in half at the cut. This should allow you to pull out the claw meat whole. If you try to break the claw with out making the cut, trust me, you will make a mess, and the meat you do get out will be full of crab shell.

Step 3. The best way to get the crab meat from the claw arm is to use the same technique used with the crab claw. The shell of the claw arm is also very hard, and almost impossible to snap in half. Place the knife in the middle of the arm and gently tap it with the mallet, stopping just short of cutting it all the way in half. After the initial cut has been made, pick up the claw arm in between your thumb and forefingers and snap it in half.

22

How to Pick (i.e., Eat) a Blue Crab

Blue crabs are prevalent where I live; other parts of the country have different types of crabs such as Dungeness, King, or Snow crabs. King crabs from Alaska are the largest, with Dungeness the next in size, and Snow crabs about six inches maximum across the shell. Blue crabs are smaller, but they are extremely tasty. It's a lot of work to pick at a dozen blue crabs, so plan on a long leisurely meal with plenty of good brew to wash it down and a bunch of good friends to help you kill the time.

Many fish stores sell already cooked crabs and your local fishmonger will tell you how to warm them up. If you can get live crabs (and they must be live to cook them), then drop the wriggling little bastards into boiling salted water (about 1 tablespoon of salt per quart). Watch out for their pincers! Boil about eight minutes per pound.

Blue crabs are generally served with a little tub of melted butter in which to dip the crab meat. Leftovers can be made into Maryland crab cakes. Since picking at blue crabs is a leisurely activity, there has arisen a whole lore and vocabulary specific to the blue crab.

Terms and Definitions
Apron—Belly/genitalia of the crab.
Backfin—White body meat including lump and large flakes (Lump + Flake = Backfin).
Buckram Crab—The stage between being a papershell and a full hard shell.
Busting—A crab that is coming out of its old shell.
Callinectes Sapidus—Scientific name for a blue crab.
Claw meat—Brownish, tougher meat from the claws.
Doublers—Two mating crabs, one on top of the other.
Flake—White body meat, other than lump.
Hardshell Crab—Have completely hardened shell. About four days after busting.
Jimmie—Male blue crab.
Keeper—A crab you can keep, about 5 inches in diameter.
Lump crab meat—Largest pieces of crab meat from the body. Located next to the back fin. It is also the most expensive and delicious form of crab meat.
Papershell—Softshells that have slightly stiffer shells.
Peelers—Blue crabs that are about to "peel" their hard outer shell. The thin new shell makes the crabs easier to eat.

Picking—The leisurely art of eating steamed blue crabs.

Pink Sign—A pink spot that appears on a crab's back fin about a week before it begins to shed its shell. The spot is the new shell beginning to show through.

She crabs—Immature female blue crabs.

Softshells—These are blue crabs that have emerged from their old shells that now have a thin soft shell.

Softshell season—Begins at the first full moon in May and continues through early fall.

Sook—Adult female blue crab.

Sponge Crab—A female crab that has an egg sack on her abdomen (pregnant crab).

About eighteen to twenty picked crabs equals 1 pound. That is why crab meat is so expensive.

What You Will Need

1. Newspapers
2. A knife
3. A mallet

Step 1. Make sure to cover your table with newspapers. Picking crabs is extremely messy.

Step 2. Place the crab on its back, with the apron facing up. Male crabs have a long slender apron, while the females have a very wide apron. You should have no problem distinguishing the two. Take a knife or your finger and pull the apron up. Bend it back and snap it off where it attaches at the rear end of the crab. Throw it away.

Step 3. Turn the crab over and put your thumb or a knife under the joint where the top and bottom of the shell meet, right where the apron snapped off. Pry off the top of the shell. Throw it away.

Step 4. With your finger or your knife, scrape away the gills. There are six gills, three on each side. Throw them away.

Step 5. Just behind the mouth is the heart, some fat, and, if the crab is a female, the eggs. These are yellow, green, and red in color. Scrape out this material, and throw it away.

Step 6. At this point you can either grab the crab on both sides and snap it in half, or use your knife and cut it right down the middle. The main objective is to have two halves.

Step 7. On each half of the crab is a membrane. Under the membrane is where the lump and flake crab meat is located. Remove the membrane with your knife or finger.

Step 8. At this point, (one at a time), grab the swimming paddles, legs, and claws and snap them off at the joint where they attach to the body. I choose to do it this way because the lump meat in the body is not attached to any of the appendages. This makes it a lot easier to remove. In many cases it can be picked out with your fingers.

Step 9. Pick out the crab meat and eat!

Removing Meat From the Claws

Step 1. Put the claw on the table with the inside of the pincers facing up. Take your knife and place it slightly behind where the pincers meet. At this point take your mallet and tap on the knife. The point of this is to make a groove in the shell and not to cut it all the way through.

Step 2. After you have put a groove in the shell, pick up the claw in both hands and carefully snap it in half at that mark. This should allow you to pull out the claw meat whole. If you try to break the claw without making the groove you will make a mess, and the meat you do get out will be full of shell. Claws are very hard to break.

Step 3. Use the same technique for the claw arm. It is also very hard, and almost impossible to snap in half. Place the knife in the middle of the arm and gently tap it with the mallet.

Some people may claim to have a better way of cleaning crabs, and each technique is as individual as the person eating them. However, the thing I love best about picking crabs is the cleanup. All you have to do is roll up the paper and throw it away. One thing I do suggest is that you put the rolled up paper in a heavy-duty trash bag. You may even want to double up. Then take the bag and place it in an outside, animal-proof trash can. Trust me, the worst smell in the world is day-old crab shells.

23

How to Eat a Lobster

Lobsters come in two basic kinds: with claws and without claws. Lobsters from the northeast coast of the United States have claws; Pacific lobsters don't. It doesn't matter, for both are delicious. Most of the meat is in the tail, and the rest is in the claws; there is also a little bit of meat inside the lobster where the legs attach. You can eat some of the inside of the lobster as well, the greenish digestive tract or the "tomalley" (liver), and in females, the unfertilized eggs ("roe" or "coral"). Don't try to eat the gills or the circulatory system, and be sure to remove the long black vein in the tail before you eat the meat.

Lobsters must be cooked while they're still alive. Most fish stores will have a tank of live lobsters, and you can pick out the one you want. Allow 1½–2 pounds per person. Boil water with 1 tablespoon of salt per quart of water. Drop the live lobster into the boiling water. Let it come to a boil again. Cover and simmer 5 minutes for the first pound and 3 more minutes each additional pound. Do not overcook. A typical 1½ pound lobster will cook in 8–10 minutes.

Lobster Terms

Carapace—Body of the lobster.

Cheliped—The name of lobster claws. The big claw is the crusher and the smaller one is used for tearing.

Roe or Coral—The unfertilized eggs in a female lobster. It will be red in color, and is also considered a delicacy.

Telsons—The small flippers at the end of the tail.

Tomalley—The green digestive tract of the lobster. Some people consider this a delicacy, however I have never have been able to get it out of my head that it is, well . . . lobster shit!

Eating the Lobster

Step 1. The first thing you want to do is to take off the legs. Grab the lobster by the back and pull off each leg with a twisting motion. Put these aside for later. If you didn't get enough to eat then you can pick at these later.

Step 2. Next you want to take the claws off. Using the same twisting motion as you did with the legs, twist the claws off at the first joint. Remove the loose claw.

Step 3. Using a nutcracker. (Lobster claws are extremely hard and a nut-cracker is the best thing to use to crack the shell.) Snap off the tip of the large section of the claw. With your finger, push the meat from the tip of the claw out the larger end that was attached to the arm.

Step 4. Next, go for the tail. Grab the tail with one hand and the back with the other. Twist the two sections until they separate.

Step 5. After you have separated the tail and the body turn the tail over. Insert your finger in to the end of the tail that was not attached to the body and force out the tail meat intact. When you have the tail meat out, peel off the top. Under the top you will find a long black vein, the digestive tract. Remove this before you eat the tail meat.

Step 6. Dip the lobster in melted butter and eat until you're stuffed.

24

How to Clean a Fish

If you're buying your fish from a fish store, just have the fishmonger do all the work. If you catch your own fish or buy them off the dock, then learning how to clean a fish is a very worthwhile endeavor. Cleaning a fish is actually pretty easy; the drawback is that if you are squeamish, it can be rather gross. Also, it can be messy. Never clean fish by a lakeside or stream; most states have laws against this, and you can be fined for doing it. Never discard the fish remains in the environment. Always throw the remains into trash containers.

First of all, make sure the fish is dead. There is nothing worse than trying to cut up something that's still moving. It will make you look real foolish. A good whack on the head with the butt end of your knife will do the job. If he's still moving, use a bigger hammer. (Just a figure of speech, hit him again harder.)

How far you go in cleaning your fish depends on the type of fish and how you want to prepare it. Some types of fish are easily deboned and can be filleted (i.e., boneless whole pieces of flesh). Salmon, bluefish, sea bass, red snapper, tuna, swordfish, and most other kinds of large sea fish and even some freshwater lake fish can easily be filleted. Trout, freshwater bass, and most freshwater stream species are generally too small to fillet and should be cooked whole. Catfish must have their skins removed before cooking (there are toxins in the skin, but the flesh is delicious). Blowfish (a saltwater fish) must have their spines removed before cooking, again because of toxins. Some species of fish can only be deboned after cooking. This is because the heat dissolves the connecting tissue between the bones and the flesh. For instance, it is easier to remove the bones from a cooked trout than from a raw one—much easier.

What You Will Need

1. Sharp knife
2. Dull knife or fish scaler
3. Trash bags
4. Appropriate place to clean fish

Step 1. Fish-Cleaning Area

The first step when cleaning a fish is to prepare your cleaning area. I emphasize this because if you leave even the smallest amount of fish scales or guts lying around, they will smell bad and attract bugs or animals. (Don't clean a fish too near your campsite or in your bathtub.)

A good way to make sure that all of the fish guts are properly disposed of is to cover your cleaning area with a plastic trash bag—that way you can just bundle it all up when you are done.

Step 2. Preparing the Outer Body of the Fish

- Wash the fish in cool water to remove excess fish oil.
- Cut off the pectoral fins with the sharp knife. (Pectoral fins—small fins attached to both *sides* of the body.)

Step 3. Scaling the Fish

- I decided to make this its own step because not all fish need to be scaled. To determine if a fish needs to be scaled take the blunt knife or scaler, apply slight pressure, and run it from the tail of the fish to the head to the fish. (Against the natural grain.) If the scales are thick and come off easily then it needs to be scaled.
- To scale a fish take a blunt knife or fish scaler and run it *from the tail to the head.*
- Repeat until the fish's body is smooth.
- Rinse the fish under cool water to remove loosened scales.

Step 4. Gutting the Fish

- Not all fish are created equal. In many cases, when cleaning a larger fish, gutting is not necessary because the meat can be cut directly off the sides. However, with small and medium sized fish gutting the fish is the only way to make sure you are getting all the meat.

- Take the sharp knife and insert it into the vent. (You guessed it, the vent is the fish's asshole. It can be found on the bottom of the fish, near the tail, where the body begins to widen.)
- Insert the knife all the way up to the top of the inside cavity just below the spine. *Do not* cut all the way through the body so that the knife is poking out of the top, you are not cutting the fish in half yet.
- Cut through the belly from the tail to the head.
- With the knife, cut out the guts and gills. (It is essential to get out the gills.)
- Open the fish like a book and scrape out any remaining guts, using a spoon or the knife. Rinse the body cavity in cool water.

Step 5. Removing the Head and Tail
- Use the sharp knife to cut the head off right below the gills.
- Cut the tail off where it meets the body—near the vent.

Filleting the Fish
- If your fish is large enough or of a species that the bones can easily be removed, you can fillet it if you like. With some species of fish you can just pull up the spine and the rib bones will come with it. Others you will have to cut through the rib bones at the spine and slide a sharp knife just under the bones and cut  them away from the meat. You should use a filleting knife (what else?), which has a long, thin, *flexible* blade.

- Open the fish like a book and cut the fish filets away from the sides of the fish, right below the dorsal fin. (The top fin that runs along the fish's back. Be careful, it can be sharp!)
- Wash your fish fillets in cool water and inspect them for bone fragments. Remove any remaining bones.
- Gather your trash bag containing the guts, bones, and gills, make sure it is properly sealed, and discard it in a trash can.
- Cook and eat!

25

How to Open a Clam

As I am sure you can imagine clams have a lot in common with their oyster brothers and sisters. They both live in salt water and they are both a pain in the ass to get open. Even though there are a lot of similarities between oysters and clams, there are some differences as well. However, since I am not a marine biologist and I don't know the scientific explanations of their differences, I am going to explain the differences between oysters and clams based on my own personal observations. Oysters taste great raw, steamed, or fried, while clams taste good steamed or fried, but in my opinion, taste nasty raw. A scientist would probably tell you that this is because non-spawning oysters contain reservoirs of glycogens (sugars) that make them taste sweeter than clams. Whatever the reason, I think they taste like crap raw. Despite the fact that I don't like them raw, many other people do. However, I really think they taste great fried, and to fry a clam you first have to get it open.

What You Will Need

1. Fresh clams
2. A clam knife, not an oyster knife—I'll explain later, keep reading
3. A sink or bucket of water

4. Heavy duty work or rubber gloves
5. Ice

Picking a Fresh Clam

Clams can be eaten year round and not just in the "R" months. Many of the same rules that apply to oysters apply to clams as well. Always buy your clams from a reputable fish store where they come from certified and inspected shellfish beds; never eat clams that are picked from uncertified beds (if you're unsure, ask to see the certification tag that comes with every bag of shellfish). While cooking will kill any bacteria, it is not certain that hepatitis is killed in the cooking process, so never, ever, eat clams from uncertified beds or ones that you've dug up yourself. Trust me on this.

The key to picking a fresh clam is to make sure they are closed tight. When clams are in standing water, they tend to open slightly to allow the water into their shells. However, if they stay open when they are handled then they are past their prime and are bad. Test clams by squeezing the shell together between your thumb and forefinger. If the shell closes tight immediately when you do this, then they are fresh and OK to eat. The one exception to this is softshelled clams, which are not eaten raw but are usually steamed. Ask your fishmonger if you are unsure.

Don't pick clams that have cracked or broken shells. When opened, clam meat should have a creamy tan color, the texture should be firm, and it should smell fresh and mild like seawater. If it smells excessively fishy or has any other kind of off odor don't eat it. If the clam is dry when opened, discard it. If the color is off (like gray, black, or red) don't eat it.

Store your clams on ice or in a refrigerator until they are ready to serve. In the fridge, cover them with a damp cloth but never put them in an airtight container or in fresh water. Make sure your clams always have plenty of ice and occasionally check them to make sure none have spoiled.

How to Open a Clam

One of the differences between oysters and clams is the way that they are opened. Oysters are opened by breaking the hinge that keeps the two pieces of the shell together. Clams are opened by slipping a skinny "clam" knife in between the two shell halves. Oysters are opened in the back, clams are opened in the front. Oyster knives are fat and blunt, used to open oysters by forcing their way through the back. Clam knives are skinny and sharp, much like paring knives with blunt points, and you have to work the knife in between the two halves of the clamshell. Trying to use an oyster shucker on a clam will not work, and a clam knife will break if you try to use it on an oyster.

Step 1. Make sure you have a well-covered and easily cleanable work station.

Step 2. Unlike oyster shells, clamshells are smooth and rounded. You are less likely to cut yourself on the shell. However, you still should put on a glove at this time to avoid cutting your hand in case your clam knife slips. Grab a clam and wash it off in your bucket of water or sink.

Step 3. Take your clam knife in your dominant hand and place the blade on the seam where the shells meet. Hold the clam parallel so that you don't spill the juices inside. Work the blade of the knife back and forth until you have worked it in between the two shell halves.

Step 4. Once you have gotten your knife between the shell halves, slowly push the knife back toward the hinge of the shell using the fingers of your *nondominant* hand on the top of the blade. Don't push the knife with your dominant hand because the blade can easily slip and cut you. Use your dominant hand as a guide. About half-way through there will be two tendons, one on each side. These tendons can be extremely strong, and difficult to cut. You may have to saw back and forth with your clam knife to cut these tendons.

Step 5. Once the two tendons have been cut, the clam will open slightly. Take your knife and cut the clam's adductor muscle away from the top shell. Cut the clam's lower adductor muscle away from the shell and twist off the top shell and discard it. You can either leave it in a shell half (hence the term "on the half shell") and serve raw on a bed of ice, or totally remove it from the shell to deep fry or use in another recipe.

The reason I didn't mention or describe how to open a roasted or steamed clam is because, unlike cooked oysters that sometimes open up due to the heat of cooking, clams always open when exposed to heat. Cooking and eating steamed clams is very easy.

Condiments

The best thing to eat steamed clams with is hot butter. For raw or fried clams serve with cocktail sauce, lemon wedges, Tabasco sauce, and horse-radish. (Use the same cocktail sauce recipe as that for oysters.)

26

How to Sharpen a Knife

I have found that the major differences you will find between your average set of good quality kitchen knives, and a $489.50 set of high quality kitchen knives is about $389.50. To get a good cut, you don't have to spend a boat-load of money on a set of knives. The difference between the two is that the higher priced knives are made of a harder metal and will stay sharper longer. This gives the illusion that they are better. Big deal. Go buy a $5 sharpening stone at your local hardware store and you will probably not be able to tell the difference between the two, and you will also have saved a couple hundred dollars.

Step 1. Buy a Sharpening Stone

Go to your local hardware store and purchase a "medium grit" sharpening stone. Buying a stone that has a finer grit is not necessary if you will only be using your knives occasionally. Sharpening stones come in several sizes ranging from about 3 inches long to up to 8–10 inches. Due to the fact that I am dealing with a sharp object and don't want to lose a finger, I stay away from the smaller ones. I prefer the middle range stones of about 5–6 inches. This way you can get a good grip on it. Buy one that is about 5–6 inches long, 1½ inches wide, and about ½ inch thick.

If the guy at the hardware store tries to get you to buy sharpening oil, claiming that it will cut down on friction, and prevent the stone from becoming clogged with steel dust from the knife, don't listen to him. The oil will only slow down the clogging of the stone from the steel dust, but it won't prevent it. If it does become a little clogged all you have to do is wash it off with water. Also, the friction between the knife and the stone is what sharpens the knife, the last thing you want to do is cut down on the friction. Sharpening oil is not necessary when sharpening everyday kitchen knives.

Step 2. Preparing Your Work Area

Since you are dealing with a sharp knife, you want to reduce the possibility of the knife or the sharpening stone slipping. If you have a workshop, with a table mounted vice, you may want to clamp down the sharpening stone. If you don't have a vice put a dishtowel on a counter and put the sharpening stone on top of it. The towel will prevent slippage, and also prevent the stone from scratching your counters.

Step 3. Positioning of the Knife

If you're right-handed, take the knife in your left hand, the edge of the blade turned *away from you* and its *tip pointing to your right.* Before you start trying to sharpen the knife, you have to angle the blade correctly. The most important aspect of sharpening a knife is the angle at which you move it across the sharpening stone. The stone should be about 15 degrees from the side of the blade, just about the thickness of the tip of your thumb between the side of the blade and the stone. (A 90-degree angle would be if the knife was right on top of the stone, forming a "T," a 0-degree angle would be if the knife were resting flat on its side against the stone.) Once you have the knife angled and positioned correctly it is time to begin sharpening.

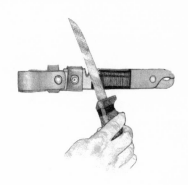

Step 4. Sharpening the Knife

After you have the proper position and angle, slowly move the knife to the right and at the same time move it up the length of the stone, away from yourself. Repeat four to five times. After a few strokes, turn the knife over, and switch hands. (The blade is still facing away from you.) Now slowly move the blade to the left, and up the length of the stone. Repeat four to five times and turn the blade back over if additional sharpening is necessary. Repeat until sharp.

Step 5. Removing the Feather Edge

When you are finished sharpening the knife there will be a "feather edge," which is loose metal that is still attached to the blade. Fold the dishtowel over a few times and run it down flat against the edge of the blade. Be careful. Repeat for both sides. Before you use the knife for cutting food make sure you wash it thoroughly. Even if you can't see it, there will be metal dust on the blade. Metal dust will quickly ruin a fine meal.

Step 6. Using a Sharpening Steel

A "sharpening" steel is really a misnomer. Only a sharpening stone can sharpen a knife. A "steel" is a device that looks like a short sword with a round blade. It can either be made of actual steel or ceramic (ceramic steels are brittle and will break if you accidentally drop them on the floor). The steel has fine grooves running the length of the round blade. When you scrape your knife edge against these grooves (again at a 15-degree angle) you align the microscopic unevenness in the knife blade to make one smooth edge. Hence the knife cuts better (but it is not really sharper). After every use of the knife, the edge will get uneven; using a steel realigns the edge.

Tips

1. Always make sure your knives are washed after their use. It is possible for bacteria to stay active on a knife blade.
2. Don't be an idiot and try to sharpen a serrated blade (like a Ginsu knife). There are special sharpeners made for serrated blades and can be bought at kitchenware stores.
3. Sharpen a knife prior to every use, it only take about two minutes. Don't try to test how sharp a knife is by slicing pieces off the person standing next to you. You will make a mess, and then have to go to jail.

27

How to Make Great Chili

In order to survive, there is only one meal that a man needs to know how to make, and that meal is chili. Chili is the staff of life. Everybody has a favorite chili recipe, some are simple and some are complex. You can make chili with just a few basic ingredients: ground beef, onions, chili powder (ground chilies, cumin, oregano, and garlic powder), and tomato sauce or puree. Most people add beans, but chili purists (snobs) point out that real chili has no beans in it. Eating is a matter of individual taste (and in the case of beans, individual digestion as well!), so do what you like. My chili recipe is complex, but I'm sure you will find it well worth the trouble.

Leftover chili can be put in microwaveable dishes and frozen for later consumption. Don't put chili in plastic containers since the fat mixed with the tomato sauce tends to permanently stain the plastic.

My Chili Recipe

The following recipe serves about 20 (or 5 football players).

1 pound	black beans, soaked overnight
3 tablespoons	bacon fat (suet)
6	garlic cloves, minced

3	large red onions, chopped small
3	medium sweet onions, chopped small
2	green peppers, chopped small
2	red peppers, chopped small
2	celery stalks, minced
3 pounds	ground beef
2 pounds	flank steak, cubed
1 pound	pork shoulder, extra lean, cubed
1 pound	Andouille sausage, chopped small (available where Cajun food is sold)
2 cups	green chiles, chopped
1 cup	Italian plum tomatoes, diced
¼ cup	parsley, minced
8 tablespoons	chili powder
2 tablespoons	ground cumin
2 tablespoons	sweet Spanish paprika
2 tablespoons	dried oregano
4	dried red peppers or 2 tablespoon crushed red pepper
2 teaspoons	black pepper, freshly ground
1 teaspoon	MSG (optional)
2 teaspoons	salt
1 teaspoon	ground coriander
2 tablespoons	Maggi seasoning (available in Asian markets)
¼ cup	Tiger sauce (available where Cajun food is sold)
16 ounces	beef broth
2 cans	tomato sauce (15 ounce each)
1 cup	tomato paste (12 ounce)
2 tablespoons	flour
12	12 ounce cans of Budweiser beer

Garnish

Diced sweet onions
Shredded cheddar or Monterey Jack cheese

Definitions of Measurements (just to be sure)

Garnish: Stuff you sprinkle on food to make it look pretty.
Simmer: Means very low heat—just hot enough to keep pot contents bubbling while covered.

Directions

Step 1. Wash the black beans and soak them in salted water overnight in the refrigerator. (Don't worry, the bean package will have directions.)

The beans should have enough water so that they are submerged in about two inches of water. The next day, cook the beans by bringing a pot of water to a boil and simmer the beans until they are tender. This usually takes 2 to 3 hours.

Step 2. Heat 2 tablespoons of bacon fat in a large skillet. Add the garlic, onions, bell peppers, and celery. Cook until the onions are clear, and the vegetables are soft. Remove the skillet from the heat and put it aside.

Step 3. Add 1 tablespoon bacon fat to the skillet and sauté the *ground* meat, cooking on medium-high heat until thoroughly browned. Drain the fat, remove the ground meat from the heat, and put it aside. Next, in the same skillet without washing it out, brown the *cubed* meats, drain the fat, and put it aside.

Step 4. Place the cooked vegetables and meats in a large pot along with the Andouille sausage. Add all remaining vegetables, spices, and liquids, *except* the beer, flour, and beans. Mix everything together a little at a time, stirring and mixing thoroughly between additions. Carefully bring the temperature up to a slow boil. Cover the chili and simmer on very low heat for approximately three to five hours. If your chili is too thin (has a lot of liquid), uncover and reduce by slowly turning up the heat. As you are cooking the chili and it is still not the desired consistency, you can also add flour (mixed smoothly in water) to thicken or the Budweiser to thin. If you use the beer to thin it out, make sure you cook the chili ½ to 1 hour more after adding the beer, so the flavor mellows. Taste and adjust for spices carefully. You will find that the flavor will develop as the chili cooks.

Step 5. Finally, about 5 minutes before serving, stir in the black beans. The beans need to be cooked separately to ensure that they do not become too mushy.

Step 6. Serve topped with chopped sweet onions and shredded cheddar or Monterey Jack cheese.

Step 7. Sit back, eat some chili, and drink the other eleven Budweisers.

PART THREE

On the Town:
A Crash Course in Eating Out

28

How to Tip

I tended bar while attending college, and believe me, either you had nice breasts or tipped well to get good service from me. In the United States we have come to think that tipping is mandatory, but in reality it is not. Tips are a bonus for an employee who has done a job well. A good server is someone who is attentive, but is not annoying. He knows the answers to your questions, yet is not too eager. (Not a kiss ass.) Since I was a bartender, and made $2.03 an hour, I know what it is like to live on tips. As a result I try to tip well. Only when there is a major mistake or incredibly bad service do I not overtip. However, since I am biased, the service rendered should dictate how much you give for a tip. Below is a guideline to how to tip for different services, and what is expected.

Occupation

Barber Cuts hair—10–20 percent of bill.

Bartender Makes and serves drinks—15 percent of tab, 20 percent if he makes exotic drinks and makes them well.

Bellman Takes bags to room, and inspects room—$1 a bag.

Caterer Provides/Serves food—15 percent of bill.

Chambermaid Cleans room—$2 a night.

Coatroom Attendant Hangs up and temporarily stores your clothing—$1 per coat/hat.

Doorman Hails cab—$1; $2 if it is raining.

Maitre D' Checks reservations, gets you into restaurant and seats you—No tip necessary. Unless you are getting into the best restaurant in town with no reservation.

Movers Moves furniture—$5–$10 per person.

Redcap Takes care of bags at train station—$1 a bag.

Rest-Room Attendant Keeps rest room clean—$1.

Shoe Shine Shines shoes—$1 for shoes; $2 for boots.

Skycap Takes care of bags at airport—$1 a bag.

Strolling Musician Sings your favorite songs—$1 tip per requested song. No requests, no tip.

Taxi Driver Drives you to your destination—10–15 percent of bill.
Valet Parks cars—$2 per car.
Waiter/Waitress Serves food—10–20 percent of bill.

Tips on Calculating Tips

If you are not a math wizard, and always hate trying to figure out how much to tip a waiter or waitress, here is a good way to figure it out. Instead of doing math, just round up the bill and move the decimal point.
Here is an example: Total Dinner Bill = $35.39

> **Step 1.** Round off the bill to make it easier to calculate.
> $35.39 = $36 (Always round up)

> **Step 2.** Move the decimal point one place to the left.
> $36 = a 10 percent tip of $3.60 (ten percent if the service is poor)

> **Step 3.** Tip according to the service. 10 percent for poor, 15 percent for average, 20 percent for great.
> If you had great service, then the tip is now $3.60 × 2 = $7.20
> If it was average, then it should be $3.60/2 = $1.80 + $3.60 = $5.40

I know, this is still math, but it does make calculating a tip a little easier.

29

How to Eat Sushi

I had my first piece of sushi a number of years ago when my brother was home on break from college. While I was still in high school, where my biggest concern was getting a date each weekend, he was studying Japanese. One night before he went back to school, my grandparents decided to take us out to dinner. Since my brother was leaving the next day, he got to choose where we ate. I know that everyone was as apprehensive as I was, but I think my brother said that since he was forced to eat peas as a child, everyone had to at least try sushi. Needless to say, our family became big sushi fans that night and I try to eat it as often as I can. My brother, on the other hand, has to eat it every day. He and his family now live in Tokyo and they helped me a lot with researching this subject. If some of the customs or terms I describe seem different than you may be accustomed to then it is because it is based on traditional Japanese etiquette.

Tip

If you decide to eat sushi, I suggest eating at a restaurant that has an actual sushi bar. The interaction with the sushi chef is just as important as the sushi itself. Sitting at the bar will provide a more enjoyable and entertaining experience than merely being served by a conventional waitress.

Sitting at the Bar

If you are going to eat at the sushi bar, try to remember that the sushi chef only fills your request for sushi. A waiter or waitress will take care of everything else. Don't insult the chef by asking him to get you another beer. Also, if you like the sushi chef, offer him a glass of beer or a cup of sake. He may not take it, but the gesture is customary and appreciated.

Once you have been seated, a waitress will come over with an *oshibori*. An *oshibori* is a steaming white hand towel that is usually presented in a basket or tray. Wipe your hands (be careful, it can be hot), then fold the towel and put it back on the tray or on the right edge of the counter. Also, if you are tired or have had a long day, it is perfectably acceptable to wipe off your face. A nice hot *oshibori* before dinner can be invigorating.

Next it is time to prepare your chopsticks or *hashi.* Almost all sushi bars have disposable *hashi* that come in a paper wrapper. Remove them from the wrapper and separate the joined pair into two sticks. In some cases the *hashi* may have a few splinters here and there. The best way to remove the splinters is to rub the *hashi* against each other in a back and forth sanding motion. In many restaurants you will find a *hashi oki* or a chopstick rest. The *hashi oki* is a small dish that is about two inches long and an inch wide. It is correct etiquette to lay the chopsticks on top of the rest so that they are parallel to the edge of the counter. If you are not provided with a *hashi oki* then you may want to make your own. Take the chop stick wrapper and fold it lengthwise in half so it makes a V-shape. Rest the eating end of the chopsticks in the center of the V so that they are not touching the counter.

Prior to ordering sushi the waitress will bring you some soy sauce, a small mixing bowl, and a green putty like substance called *wasabi.* Even though this substance looks like avocado, or some type of cucumber paste, it is not. What it is, is a form of *very* spicy horseradish. Whatever you do, *do not* eat it in this form, the wasabi is to be mixed with the soy sauce. Trust me, even if you like spicy food, don't try to be cool and taste the *wasabi* without mixing it with soy sauce or you will be very sorry. Pour about one to two teaspoons of soy sauce into the mixing bowl, and using one of your chopsticks as a knife/spoon type utensil, mix a *small* amount of the *wasabi* in with the soy sauce. Mix thoroughly. Taste your mixture, and continue to add soy sauce or *wasabi* until you have arrived at your desired spiciness. Many types of nigiri sushi (sliced seafood on a dollop of sticky rice) have wasabi tucked under the fish already, you may want to check before adding more.

Choosing Sushi

Sushi menus will always vary, but there will be a few items that can almost always be found at a sushi restaurant. (It's like buffalo wings at a sports bar, you know that they will be on the menu.) Most sushi bars will also have diagrams, pictures, or charts for non-Japanese speaking customers, and the sushi chef will probably speak English too. I recommend asking him for his opinion. Making good sushi is not like flipping burgers at the local diner; it is a time honored tradition and sushi chefs take their work seriously. If raw fish is not your thing then you should know that of all of the sushi bars I have been to, I have never been to one that didn't offer a type of sushi that doesn't contain raw fish. There are many different types of vegetable rolls. The most common is known as a *California Roll*. A California roll is maki sushi with avocado and cucumber.

Types of Sushi

1. **Maki Sushi** A rolled sushi consisting of a combination of rice, vegetables, or raw fish. You probably picture this type of sushi when sushi is mentioned. Tekka Maki is tuna; Kappa Maki is cucumber; Futo Maki are giant rolls.
2. **Nigiri Sushi** Hand-formed rice with a slice of seafood, usually raw fish, place on top of the rice.
3. **Inari Sushi** A soybean pouch filled with lightly sweetened sushi rice.
4. **Temaki Sushi** Hand-rolled sushi. It is described as looking like an ice cream cone. This type of sushi can be difficult to eat, and it is hard to share. My sister-in-law says it is a rip-off and to not even bother with it.
5. **Chirashi Sushi** A bowl of sushi rice topped with vegetables or seafood.

If you are served raw fish that is not accompanied by rice, it is not sushi; it is *sashimi. Sashimi* means raw fish in Japanese.

Fish or Seafood Commonly Used in Sushi and Sashimi

Salmon (*Sake*) Has a soft pink color.
Salmon Roe (*Ikura*) Red bubbles about ¼ inch in diameter.
Tuna (*Maguro*) Dark pink or red color.
   (*Toro*) A fatty tuna that looks almost like salmon. It has white lines of fat running through it.

Mackerel (*Saba*) White.

Eel (*Unagi;* **Ocean Eel**-*Anago*) Eel is not eaten raw, but is roasted and is dark brown in color.

Shrimp (*Ebi*) Pink color, shrimp is cooked, not raw.

Sweet Shrimp (*Ama Ebi*) Raw shrimp.

Yellow Tail (*Hamachi*) Off-white with reddish brown edges. Rich and buttery.

Octopus (*Taco*) Rubbery, white and purple, also tough.

Red Snapper (*Tai*) Translucent white with pink edges.

Squid (*Ika*) Rubbery white, like bubble gum that grows in your mouth.

How to Eat Sushi Properly

If you're wondering if I'm going to tell you some ancient Japanese secret, you are mistaken. When your sushi is served, pick up a piece with your chopsticks, give it a quick dip in the soy sauce/wasabi mixture, and pop the whole piece in your mouth. Sushi is designed to be eaten in one bite, and should be small enough where you don't have a problem adhering to this custom. It may be difficult for some people to eat an entire piece in one bite. If you are ordering and sharing sushi with others (on a group platter) it is considered polite to flip you chopsticks around and pick pieces off the community plate with the handle ends. It is also rude to touch rice to the soy sauce mixture. Instead flip the sushi upside down and touch the fish side to the soy sauce. You can also remove the raw fish from the rice, dunk it, and put it back on top, then eat. It is also perfectly polite to eat sushi with your fingers, this is considered much better than dropping rice in the soy sauce bowl.

When you have finished with one type of sushi, and want to try a different type, Japanese cleanse their pallet by eating small pieces of pink pickled ginger called *gari*. Cleansing your pallet means getting rid of any lingering taste in your mouth by eating something that flushes the sinuses and taste buds.

Extras

In addition to raw fish and vegetables, some sushi bars will offer other types of traditional Japanese foods:

Miso Soup A warm broth, made from bean curd. It can be plain or contain chunks of tofu or vegetables as well. Feel free to sip the soup directly from the bowl or pick up the bowl with one hand and use your chopsticks with the other. It is also OK to slurp.

Tofu White cubes about 1-inch square made out of soybeans. Either served in miso soup or fried in batter and served hot (*Agedahi Dofu*) Actually very tasty.

Salads Greens usually consist of cucumber strips seasoned with white vinegar.

Tsukemono Bite-size pickles.

Edamame Whole cooked soybeans similar to peanuts.

Oshinko Pickled radish.

30

How to Use Chopsticks

I used to think that using chopsticks was a pain in the ass. They are cumbersome and weird, and it just didn't make a whole lot of sense when you could use a fork. However, I have found out that if you learn how to use them correctly it will make your dining experience more meaningful and often more enjoyable. Look at it this way, if you went to a 3-D movie and you didn't wear the 3-D glasses, you still saw the movie—right? Well, you did, but you didn't get the full experience. Using chopsticks when eating a Japanese meal is the same thing. It just makes it better. If you are in Japan and should request a fork and a knife, then they will probably refer to you as a *gaijin,* our equivalent of being called a dumbass.

How to Hold and Use Chopsticks

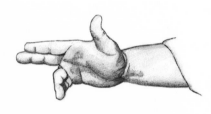

Step 1. First, stick your hand out as if it were a gun, but instead of sticking out just one finger as the barrel of the gun, use both the index and middle fingers.

Step 2. Second, move your ring and pinky fingers perpendicular to the middle and index fingers. (Your ring and pinky fingers will form a 90 degree angle. Keep your thumb sticking up.) I didn't say this was easy.

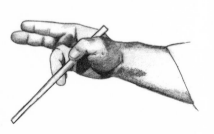

Step 3. Third, lay a chopstick across the web of your hand (in between your thumb and index finger) and the tip of your middle finger. The tip of your middle finger should be in the middle of the chopstick. Hold it in place with your thumb. This chopstick will remain stationary, and you will use the other stick as a lever, to pick up food.

Step 4. Next, while still holding the first chopstick, put the second chopstick on top of it and hold the second chopstick as if it were a pencil, between your thumb and index finger. Use your middle finger for support. Pretend you are writing, and move the second chopstick back and forth to get the hang of it. It takes time to get used to, but once you have it down you will catch on quick.

In addition to actually using chopsticks, there are some other basic rules of etiquette that you should know when eating at a Japanese restaurant. First, when you are not using them, don't store your chopsticks vertically in your rice bowl. It is like sticking your fork into your steak and leaving it there. This is considered a serious insult. Second, don't pass items between people using only chopsticks, put it on their plate. Third, when taking food from a communal dish, turn the chopsticks upside down and use the part that has not been in your mouth to pick up items. Finally, don't use your chopsticks as a conducting wand, drumsticks, or as a pointer. The Japanese probably won't care if you do this, but it will just make you look stupid.

Spoons are used when eating soups primarily consisting of broth, such as miso soup, however, if the soup contains noodles, it is expected that you use your chopsticks to eat them. Also, don't worry about noises, slurping when eating soup and noodles is commonplace, but to avoid making a mess lift the soup bowl to just below your mouth. Even in America this will not be considered bad manners in a Japanese restaurant. Considering that the Asian culture is centuries old, there are a number of etiquette rules that may be appropriate for different situations. I recommend that if you ever have any reservations about how to eat without offending anyone, try to follow the lead of others eating around you. Watch and learn.

Tip

You can tell if you are eating at a good Asian restaurant if there are other Asians eating there.

31

How to Match Food With Wine

Out of all the *how tos* I researched for this book, "How to Match Food With Wine" was by far the hardest to write. Every wine shop manager or wine connoisseur had his own theories and rules; by the time I finished talking to someone, I was ten times more confused than when I first started. I finally realized that, in today's world of ten thousand different wines, the first rule of matching wine with food is that there are no rules. Let me explain by example: I remember that when I was in elementary school you could buy milk to drink with your lunch, it cost 8 cents, and your choices were regular vitamin D or skim. Today elementary schools offer: skim milk, vitamin D milk, 2% milk, chocolate milk, skim chocolate milk, lactose-free milk, etc. Get the picture? It is the same thing with wine. There are so many varieties of wine today that it is hard to say what type of wine goes with what type of food.

Nevertheless, I hope to provide you with some general guidelines that will help you chose a wine, but the best advice I can give is to use your common sense and follow your instincts. One wine shop owner told me that you should pick a wine that you like to drink by itself. The reason for this he said was that he usually drank a majority of his wine either before or after dinner. He did drink wine during dinner, but he said he drank water too. He said jokingly that, even if the food stinks, at least you know you will have a good wine to drink.

For most of you the Level 1 Wine Rules should suffice until you gain more experience or want to experiment.

Wine Rules: Level 1

The "I Want to Make a Good Impression, but Don't Know What I am Doing" Level.

1. White wine goes with white meats—fish, chicken, and seafood.
2. Red wine goes with red meats and pasta with red sauce.
3. Serve a hearty, heavier wine with a heavier meal.
4. Serve a lighter wine with a lighter meal.

Wine Rules: Level 2

The "Freshman at an Ivy League School" Level.

1. Don't serve wine with salad.
2. Don't serve wine with eggs.

3. Don't serve wine with chocolate.
4. Drink red wine with cheese.
5. Drink a lighter red wine with pork and lamb.
6. Drink a light white wine with a vegetarian or meatless meal.

Wine Rules: Level 3

The "James Bond" Level.

1. Drink champagne with caviar.
2. Drink Cabernet Sauvignon with steak.
3. Drink Chianti with pasta and red sauce.

Wine Rules: Level 4

The "Snotty Ex-wife of a Fortune 500 CEO" Level.

1. If you are serving wine alone, serve a red wine, but serve something young and fruity.
2. If you are serving fish, a red or white is OK, but avoid oaky whites and tannic reds.
3. Serve a light red wine with shellfish.
4. Serve white wine with white meats in a cream sauce.
5. "Browned" white meats can be served with red wine.
6. "Rare" red meats can be served with white wine.
7. Serve Cabernet Sauvignon with lamb.
8. Serve Pinot Noir or Burgundy with roast beef.

The Pecking Order of Wines

1. Drink younger wine before you drink older wine.
2. Drink white wine before you drink red.
3. Drink dry wines before sweet wines.

32

How to Order Wine

If you don't have a lot of experience with wine it is easy to feel like a zit-faced kid on his first date when the waiter asks you if you would like to order some wine. I remember the first time the waiter gave me a wine cork. I thought he was giving it to me as a momento of my date, I didn't know what he wanted me to do with it.

When ordering wine the first rule is don't stress out about it. The job of the waiter is to help you make a decision, and if you have any questions just ask. In general, if you are not a wine connoisseur, then you should know that there are three basic rules when ordering wine in a restaurant.

Rules

1. Have a predetermined price range.
2. Ask the waiter—it's his job to know.
3. Stick with what you know.

Even if the thought of ordering wine from a wine list makes you break out in a cold sweat, here is a good script you can use:

WAITER: Would you like to order some wine?
CUSTOMER: Yes, I would, but I am not sure exactly what to get. I am thinking about having the tuna special, have any suggestions?
WAITER: We have a great house Chardonay that is excellent with the tuna. Would you like to try that?
CUSTOMER: How is that served, by the glass or the bottle?
WAITER: It is served both ways—$4.50 a glass and $18.95 a bottle.
CUSTOMER: Sounds good. Let's go ahead and start with a bottle.

If you are still nervous about ordering wine in a restaurant and don't think you can memorize the above script, then order a beer and forget about it.

A Wine Ritual

After you have ordered your wine, the waiter will bring you the bottle for your inspection. The historic purpose of this is to allow the customer to check the label and the vintage of the wine you have ordered. The waiter will next uncork the bottle and present you with the cork. The presentation of a wine bottle's cork dates back hundreds of years, when there were no actual labels on wine bottles. Due to the fact that some restaurants would try to pass off cheap French wine as expensive wine, wineries used to brand the actual corks as proof of where the wine originated. Waiters used to present diners with the bottle's cork as proof of where the wine originated. This practice continues today, although it is not really necessary. Inspect the cork for mold or crystallization; if either is present reject the bottle and ask for a new one. Don't even bother to taste the wine if the cork has mold, crystals, or smells of vinegar. The waiter will then pour you a small taste, waiting for you to approve the selection before serving everyone else. Taste it, and if it's OK, nod to the waiter to finish pouring.

PART FOUR

Holding Your Liquor:
A Crash Course in Alcohol

33

Wine Definitions

There are millions of books, magazines, clubs, experts, newsletters, snobs, and web pages that all pertain to wine. If you learn the following definitions and pronunciations, you should be able to hold a conversation with a wine enthusiast or possibly limp your way through a wine tasting.

White Wine

Chardonnay (SHAR-doe-nay) Based on the number of bottles sold, Chardonnay is the world's most popular white wine. It is a dry wine that is medium to full-bodied. It usually has an apple or citrus flavor, but it can sometimes taste buttery due to the aging in oak barrels. It is good served with simple seafood and poultry.

Chenin Blanc (SHEN-in Blonk) Its popularity has declined somewhat in recent years. It is a light, fruity wine that often has a fruity aroma and flavor. (Think melon, apple, peach, or apricot.) It is a good wine by itself or with casual meals.

Gewürztraminer (Guh-VERTZ-tra-meener) A German wine. The spicy flavors are ideal with ham, pork, sausages, or spicy Asian food. Its aromas and flavors have been compared to peaches, grapefruits, and allspice.

Muscat (MUSS-cat) A wine that is best served with desserts of fresh fruit. It has a very floral, apricot-like aroma and flavor.

Riesling (REES-ling) Also a German wine that has a flowery/appleish aroma. Rieslings range from slightly to very sweet and can be either a table or dessert wine. Dry Rieslings go well with chicken, pork, and spicy foods.

Sauvignon Blanc (SO-vin-yawn BLONK) A lighter wine than Chardonnay. Has a citrus and herbal aroma and flavor. It is a versatile wine that can be served with shellfish, fish, chicken, pasta, and Caesar salad.

Red Wines

Barbera (Bar-BEAR-a) A classic Italian red wine that has black cherry and plum flavors. It has a silky texture and its acidity is good to match with tomato sauces. Similar to Merlot.

Cabernet Sauvignon (CA-burr-nay SO-vin-yawn) This is considered the king of red wines. It is full bodied with rich currant flavors. It is best served with simple beef or lamb dishes.

Grenache (Gra-NOSH) Grown in Spain, South of France and California. Grenache is usually blended with other grape varieties, has a light color, and has a citrus character. Good with lighter meats.

Merlot (Mare-LOW) Merlot is similar to Cabernet but it has a softer and fruitier flavor and aroma. It can have hints of cherry, mint, or tobacco.

Pinot Noir (PEE-know Na-WAHR) More delicate than Cabernet or Merlot. It can have a fruity, strawberry, or tea aroma and flavor. Good with grilled salmon, grilled lamb, or roasted chicken.

Sangiovese (San-gee-oh-VAY-zee) A medium bodied wine that has berry, plum, or floral aromas. It is a good match for light Italian or Mediterranean style foods.

Syrah (Sah-RAH) A hearty, spicy red. It has fruity aromas, and hints of pepper. It is great with steaks, wild game, and stews.

Zinfandel (ZIN-fan-dell) The world's most versatile wine grape. It has a zesty berryish flavor that goes well with tomato sauces and grilled meats.

34

Beer Definitions

When I was growing up you could still buy beer when you were eighteen years old, and the biggest decision you had to make was whether to buy crappy light beer or crappy regular beer. At the local 7-Eleven there was maybe one freezer dedicated to cold beer—the rest was warm and sat in the back hallway near the bathrooms and the mop bucket. If this book were written ten to fifteen years ago, I probably wouldn't have included this section, because there may have only been a handful of definitions that would have been needed to cover a majority of the beer on the market. Today, on the other hand, it is not uncommon to have a microbrewery right up the street, or a local bar that boasts having the city's widest selection of beer on tap. The reason I personally like microbreweries so much is because I like the way the bartenders look at me when I ask for a Budweiser. They look at me as if I am speaking a foreign language.

Traditionally, beer can be divided into two types: ales, which use top fermenting yeast, and lagers, which use bottom fermenting yeast. The water, types of malt, the type of yeast strain, the types of hops, and the brewing procedure all define the differences between beers. Ales include: Stout, Porter, Pale Ale, Brown Ale, and Barley Wine. Lagers include: Bock, Pilsner, Cream Ale, and German Style Ale.

Ale The name given to a beer that is fermented at warmer temperature 60–77°F, 18–25°C and quicker (3–5 days). Ales are usually made in open brewing kegs and the yeast floats on top of the beer. Ale covers a broad spectrum of beer and not all have the same characteristics: bitter, brown ale, pale ale, red ale, porter, and stout.

Barley Of the five cereal grains used for malting (corn, rice, wheat, rye, and barley) barley is the best. Barley's husk protects it from mold growth and also serves as a filter during wort (the malt and hop mixture) separation. During the malting process, the starches in the barley are broken down into their component sugars: dextrin and maltose. Next, during the fermentation process, maltose is converted into alcohol and carbon dioxide while dextrin adds to the flavor of the beer.

Barley Wine Even though barley wine tastes as strong as wine, it is in no way related to wine. Rather the term barley wine is an English term for very strong "ale." The way brewers get the higher alcohol content is by adding more malt and then leaving the brews in their kegs for several months (instead of days or weeks).

Beer Beer is an alcoholic beverage traditionally made from malted grains (barley, wheat, corn, and rice) hops, yeast, and water. Beer has two categories, ale and lager.

Bitter Bitter is a style of "ale" that has a strong taste and after taste of hops. Bitter is usually a gold or copper red color, and originally every brewery in England had two types of ales, a bitter and mild. Bitter is stronger, dryer, and hoppier than other ales.

Bock Bock is a very strong beer and the term bock means "billy goat" in German. The accepted theory as to how it got its name is that the word "bock" is a derivation from "Einbeck" and Einbeck is the name of the town where bock style beer originated. It is usually served between Christmas and May and it comes in a variety of styles, ranging from pale to the traditional dark color. Double bocks are even stronger than single bocks, and they also vary in taste from well-balanced to an overwhelming maltiness.

Brown Ale A British-style ale with a mild, flavorful taste. It also has a lower than average alcohol content.

Cream Ale Cream ale is an ale brewed at a lower temperature using hops of traditional lagers. Even though it is an ale, because of the brewing process it takes on some of the smoothness and taste of lager.

Draught Beer This type of beer is served directly from the barrel, cask, or keg through a tap. Even though some beer brewers claim to have draught beer taste in a bottle or can, draught beer always tastes different than when it is served from the handy single-serve container.

Dry Beer Dry beer is a type of beer brewed with more additives, like corn or rice. It also uses a type of yeast that ferments the wort more completely. The beer that is produced has less flavor, but also less aftertaste. Dry beers are suggested to people who don't like strong tasting beers with complex flavors.

Eisbock Also called ice bock. It is a style of bock beer developed in Germany where the beer is allowed to partially freeze. The ice chunks are then removed and the resulting brew has a higher alcohol content and less of an aftertaste.

Export Export is a gold-colored lager that is dryer than a Munich-style lager, and is less hoppy than a pilsner, but it is also stronger than both. It was originally produced in Dortmund and is sometimes known as "Dort."

Firkin A firkin is a medium-sized beer keg that has a capacity of 40.9 liters or 10.8 US gallons.

Hefe The German word for yeast. It means a sedimented beer.

Hops Hops are the unpollinated flower from the female hop vine. Different varieties of hops add different flavors, aromas, and different levels of bitterness to beer. Hops also acts as a natural preservative. Strong hops are added at different times during the brewing process, while milder hops are brewed in a massive hop percolator and added to the beer near the end of the brewing process.

Ice Beer Ice beer is created the same way as eisbock. The temperature of the beer is lowered so that the water in the beer begins to freeze. The ice chunks are then filtered out, resulting in a beer with a higher alcohol content.

International Bitterness Units (IBU's) IBU's are the measurement of the bite that is given by the hops in the beer. Most large mass-produced beers have IBU's of about 10–15, while microbreweries have IBU's in the 25–35 range.

Lager A general term for a beer that is fermented in cold temperatures 8–10°C (45–50°F) where the yeast fermenting at the bottom of the brewing tank. Lager comes from the German word *lagern* meaning to store. The reason for this name is because lagers are fermented at cold temperatures for two weeks then they are "lagered" or stored for up to three months at a temperature that is near freezing. Lagers include names like pilsner and bock.

Lambic Ale Lambics are most often found in Belgium, and they get their taste by exposing the wort (malt and hop mixture) to outside air. The exposure of the wort allows other microorganisms and wild yeast strains to mix in with the fermenting beer. Fruit is also sometimes added.

Light Beer A watered-down pilsner that has little taste and a light yellow color. It is a term that originated in America. Some light beer brands, rather than water-down the beer, use special enzymes that ferment most of the carbohydrates out of the beer.

Malt Malt refers to a malted grain, and in most beers barley is the main grain used. The malting process can be defined as when barley is exposed to warmth and moisture long enough to cause it to begin to sprout. This process converts the grain starch into fermentable sugars that combine with the yeast to produce the alcohol.

Malt Liquor A pale golden-colored, strong lager with a medium body that is usually cheaply made and consumed in the United States. It will get you really drunk, make you act mean, and give you one hell of a hangover.

Märzen Märzen beer or March beer gets its name from the time when brewers brewed a large batch of beer that would last from March to October. It is also considered the traditional beer of Octoberfest. It is amber red and has a medium to strong strength. The maltiness is present in the bouquet, but it is not overpowering.

Munich Helles and Munich Dunkel The helles is a golden-colored pale lager. It is less hoppy than a pilsner and malt accented. The dunkel is a malty dark lager.

Pale Ale, India Pale Ale, or IPA IPA is super premium pale ale that has a very high hop content. The reason IPA was originally made with a high hop content was that it was a beer that was going to be exported to India. To keep it from going bad on the long journey brewers increased the hop content. Pale ale has a malty character yet you can also taste the fruitiness of the yeast. It is a copper-colored ale from England and is characterized by a dry and hoppy finish.

Pilsner Pilsner was first brewed in 1842 in the Bohemian brew town of Pilsen. It quickly became very popular, especially in Germany, and has been imitated throughout the world. In America, pilsner is used to describe any golden colored beer, but the mass produced versions have little resemblance to the original pilsner. Pilsner is a premium pale lager with a classic gold color. The bouquet is flowery and fragrant, while the finish is dry and hoppy.

Porter Porter is a style of ale. It is also a dark top-fermenting beer that originated in London and it is known for having a dry yet balanced hoppiness. It was the drink of choice in the eighteenth and nineteenth century, and has become popular in more recent years with the growing popularity of microbreweries. Its general characteristics are a strong flavor, very dark color, and a high hoppiness.

Red Ale A red ale is a moderately hoppy medium body Irish-style ale that has a flavorful taste.

Reinheitsgebot This is the Bavarian beer purity law of 1516 that says that only barley, water, and hops were allowed in beer. You may have heard this term used in a Sam Adams beer commercial. The modern *Reinheitsgebot* adds one further ingredient: yeast, something they didn't know about in 1516.

Scotch Ale Scotch ale uses black malt that gives the color and dryness. It is a full-bodied ale that has a malty character. They are usually not hopped as highly as English ales.

Steam Beer Steam beer is a lager fermented at a higher temperature, similar to the way ale is brewed. It has some of the fruity characteristics of an ale, but also has the body of a lager. The style was developed in the late 1800's in San Francisco and is called steam beer because when the fermenting kegs were opened, releasing the carbon dioxide, it looked like steam.

Stout The most widely known type of stout is Irish stout. It is dryer and has a more intense flavor than English stouts. Its characteristics are a very dark color, strong flavor, and a rich, creamy head. Stout is a style of ale.

Weisse beer or Weizen beer It's made from wheat and is generally a light flavorful beer, although there are dark weizen beers. It is served in a very tall glass with a slice of lemon or a shot of raspberry syrup.   .

Wort Wort is the name of the liquid that will become beer once yeast is added. Wort is created by mashing the malted grains, boiling the resulting malt liquor, and adding hops.

Yeast Yeast is a single celled organism that is actually related to fungus. Related yeasts are used to also make bread, or wine, and there are different types of yeast that are available for making beer. Ale yeast is known as *Saccharomyces cerevisiae* and lager yeast is *Saccharomyces uvarum* or *S. carlsbergensis*. The ale yeast multiplies rapidly in warm wort, while the lager yeast multiplies slowly in cold wort. The yeast consumes the sugar in the wort and converts it into alcohol and carbon dioxide.

35
Liquor Definitions

Gin

Gin was invented in the seventeenth century by a doctor from Holland named Franciscus Sylvius. The doctor originally prescribed gin as a medicine, and it became very popular with British soldiers who were involved in various skirmishes in the area. The name "gin" is a derivation of the French word for one of the main ingredients, juniper berries.

Gin is made by adding juniper berries, as well as other flavorings to grain neutral alcohol. It is a very distinct liquor, and there can be a big difference between different brands. The differences usually depend on the "other" ingredients added in the mixing process. People either love or hate gin, and unlike whiskey or tequila it is usually not imbibed in shot form. So if you ever see anyone take a shot of gin, then they are probably very drunk, just plain dumb, or have dead taste buds.

Vodka

Vodka comes from Eastern Europe and the word "vodka" is Russian meaning "little water." It was used as medicine in the Middle Ages and called *zhiznennia voda* meaning "water of life." How appropriate! It is a neutral liquor that is distilled from a variety of grains, but unlike gin, it is filtered so that impurities are removed and all that remains is a neutral liquor. US law states that colors, flavors, and impurities must be filtered from all brands of vodka. The flavors in flavored vodkas, such as lemon or hot pepper, are added after the distillation process. Even though some vodka drinkers swear that they can tell differences in the different brands of vodka, in many cases, if the vodka is of the same quality, it will be hard to tell any two brands apart. As a result, I suggest that if you are drinking a mixed drink where the taste of the vodka is canceled out by the drink's other ingredients, such as a Bloody Mary or White Russian, it is a waste to spend money on a premium-brand vodka. Trust me, you will not be able to tell the difference. However, if you are drinking a drink with lighter mixers, such as a Vodka Tonic or Vodka Martini, I recommend a premium blend. Higher quality brands may not taste different, but they can be a lot smoother.

Whiskey

Scotch Whiskey or Scotch Originated in Scotland, and has a very wide range of characters, blends, and personalities. The flavor of Scotch primarily comes from the smoked malted barley that is used in the fermenting process. The biggest difference you will find in Scotch is if it is made with a "single malt" or if it is a "blend" of different grains. The single malts use only one type of barley, while blended Scotches use a mixture of malted, unmalted barley, and other grains. Single-malt Scotch is considered to be the best, with premium brands aging twelve years or more.

Irish Whiskey Guess where this comes from? Irish whiskey is very much like Scotch; the main difference is that Scotch distilleries use fires made with peat to roast their barley. The peat gives Scotch a smoky flavor with hints of iodine. The barley used in Irish whiskey is roasted in kilns (big ovens), and Irish whiskey usually has a sweeter and sharper flavor than Scotch.

Canadian Whiskey Canadian whiskey is a blend of flavorful and neutral whiskeys, resulting in a rather straightforward, smooth, and light taste. Canadian whiskey is widely used in mixed drinks.

Bourbon Bourbon was born in Bourbon County, Kentucky, a long time ago. Nobody is exactly sure when it was first made because the inventors were so drunk no one bothered to write it down. Just kidding. The main ingredient in bourbon is corn, but it usually also contains a variety of other grains. Other than the corn used in the distilling process, bourbon gets its distinctive taste from the wooden barrels in which it is commonly aged. Premium bourbon is barrel aged for twelve years or more.

Rye Rye is similar to bourbon only that instead of corn, it is made with rye. Rye used to be a very popular liquor, but it is also known to be very strong and harsh. Let me put it this way, if you are ordering a drink and the bartender ask if you want rye or bourbon, go with the bourbon. Old one-legged sailors drink rye.

Rum Rum originated in the Caribbean and its primary ingredient is also the area's largest export—sugar cane. Rum is actually a very diverse beverage that has a lot of different styles and flavors. The finer rums, like the better bourbons and Scotches are aged for ten years or more. Since the major ingredient in rum is sugar cane, and alcohol is made when sugar breaks down in the fermentation process, rum retains more of its elemental taste than any other liquor. Rum is unique in that it shares some of the characteristics of vodka, such as its neutrality. Yet, it also shares some of the distilling features of Scotch and bourbon. For example, the longer it is aged the better it is. There is dark rum (made with molasses), light rum, añejo (aged), spiced, and gold rums. Even though rum is a unique and flavorful liquor, most people have stereotyped rum as being a cheap liquor used in a wide variety of fruity and specialty Caribbean drinks. Since real men don't drink fruity drinks, rum has been given a bad rap. Ever see a biker order a Mai Tai?

Tequila Tequila comes from the agave plant, which is found in a region of Mexico surrounding the town of Tequila. It is a double distilled alcohol and if bottled directly from the distillery is clear and known as "white" tequila. "Gold" tequila, named for its color, is aged in oak barrels, and develops into a smoother more complex liquor the longer it ages. Just like rum, tequila is also known for its mixed drinks, such as Frozen Margaritas, Tequila Sunrises, etc. However, the most popular way of drinking this liquor is in "shot" form. Shooting tequila can be accredited to the Mexican hero Pancho Villa, which just happened to be his favorite way to drink the infamous liquor. Mr. Villa would take a lime wedge in his hand, then lick the small indentation between his thumb and forefinger of that same hand, pour a small amount of salt there, then in quick succession: lick the salt, down the shot, and bite into the lime wedge. He would then bang down the shot glass with some authority and yell out, "Tonight we ride." (Actually, I don't know if he said that, but it sounds good.)

36

Bar Tools and Glasses

Glassware is not as important as the actual ingredients in your drinks, but you should know the terminology and which drinks are served in which glasses. There are dozens of different types of glasses, some used specifically for individual drinks. (Such as a martini glass or a daiquiri glass.) Here are the basics:

Collins Glass This glass has several different names, which depends on the drink that is served in it. This larger glass can range from 10–14 oz. and is used for larger mixed or tropical drinks. Daiquiri, Piña Colada, Zombie, Long Island Iced Tea, etc.

Garnish Fruit or vegetable added to a drink to enhance the flavor and presentation.

Highball Glass This glass is probably the one you will use the most. It can range from 8–12 oz. And they are used for mixed drinks such as Gin and Tonics, Bourbon and Coke, Screwdrivers, Tequilas Sunrises, etc.

Jigger A 1½ oz glass or metal cup used to measure liquor—basically, a shot glass.

Muddle To mash and stir. In an Old-Fashioned the sugar and fruit is muddled together before the liquor is added.

Rocks Means serve with ice.

Rocks Glass The rocks glass is also called an old-fashioned glass, lowball glass, or a sour glass. Can range from 4–6 oz. Used for Old-Fashioneds, White Russians, Whiskey Sours, and various whiskey rocks combinations.

Shooter A drink meant to be downed in a single shot, for example, Sex on the Beach or a Kamakazi.

Shot Glass 1½ oz. glass that is used for shots and measuring.

Spritzer A 50/50 combination of white wine and club soda.

Straight Up or Up A mixed drink served without ice.

Top Shelf The next time you are in a bar, take a look at how the liquor is arranged. In almost every bar I have been in, the liquors are on different shelves and on different levels. On the bottom shelf are the cheaper liquors, while the top shelf is reserved for the premium liquors. The term "top shelf" refers to any drink that is made with premium liquors taken from the top shelf.

37

Drink Recipes

There are thousands of drink variations and bar tools that are use in the preparation of alcoholic beverages. The following is a list of the most popular recipes.

Bloody Mary

1½ ounce vodka
4 ounces tomato juice
½ teaspoon Worcestershire sauce
½ teaspoon lemon juice
Several drops of Tabasco sauce
½ teaspoon horseradish (optional)
Salt and pepper
Celery stalk

Shake well over ice and strain into a highball glass. Add ice cubes and garnish with a celery stalk.

Cape Cod

2 ounces vodka
Cranberry juice
Lime wedge

Put three ice cubes into a highball glass. Pour in the vodka. Fill the glass with cranberry juice, stir, and serve in a highball glass. Garnish with the lime wedge.

Cosmopolitan

1 ounce vodka
½ ounce Triple Sec
½ ounce Rose's Lime Juice
½ ounce cranberry juice
Lime wedge

Shake liquid ingredients like hell in a shaker with ice. Place lime wedge on the rim of a Martini glass. Pour mix into the glass, up (i.e., without ice). Enjoy!

Daiquiri

2 ounces light rum
1 ounce lime juice
1 teaspoon sugar
Lime slice

Shake well with crushed ice and strain into a chilled Collins glass. Garnish with a slice of lime.

Gimlet

2 ounces gin
½ ounce lime juice
Lime twist

Pour the gin and lime juice over ice in a shaker. Strain into a cocktail glass, garnish with a lime twist or lime slice.

Gin and Tonic or Vodka and Tonic

2 ounces gin or vodka
5 ounces tonic water
Lime wedge

Pour gin and tonic into a highball glass that is about half-way filled with ice cubes. Stir well and garnish with the lime wedge.

Kamikaze

1½ ounce vodka
½ ounce Triple Sec
½ ounce lime juice
Mix together with crushed ice, strain into a cocktail glass, and drink. This can also be consumed as a shooter.

Long Island Iced Tea

¾ ounce vodka
¾ ounce gin
¾ ounce white rum
¾ ounce white tequila
¾ ounce Triple Sec
1 ounce lemon juice or Tom Collins mix
Dash of Coke

Stir ingredients with ice and strain into a Collins glass filled with ice. All liquors should be clear. It should actually taste like iced tea with a kick.

Mai Tai

1 ounce light rum
½ ounce Orgeat syrup (almond-flavored syrup)
½ ounce grenadine syrup
½ ounce Triple Sec
1½ ounce sweet and sour mix
Maraschino cherry

Shake all ingredients (except the cherry) with ice and strain into a Collins glass over several ice cubes. Top with a cherry and serve.

Manhattan

2 ounces Canadian whiskey, Irish whiskey, or bourbon
½ ounce sweet vermouth
Dash of Angostura bitters
Maraschino cherry
Dash cherry juice

Shake with cracked ice and strain into a chilled cocktail glass. Serve with a maraschino cherry. For a sweeter Manhattan add a little cherry juice.

"Top Shelf" Margarita

1½ ounce Cuervo 1800 Tequila
½ ounce Grand Marnier
½ ounce Rose's Lime Juice
Splash of sour mix
1 tablespoon egg white. The egg white adds body and froth to the
    Margarita.

Mix together, shake vigorously for 30 seconds, serve in a salt-rimmed highball glass.

The Perfect Martini

1½ ounce gin
1 teaspoon dry vermouth
1 teaspoon sweet vermouth
1 olive

Stir gin and vermouth over ice in a shaker. Strain into a Martini glass, add the olive, and serve. There are several variations of a Martini that are due to the amount and type of vermouth used. If someone asks for a dry

Martini, only use dry vermouth. If someone asks for a Gibson make a dry Martini and serve with pearl onions. Martinis can also be made with vodka.

Old-Fashioned

1 teaspoon sugar
2 dashes Angostura bitters
Splash of club soda
Orange wedge
2 ounces bourbon
Maraschino cherry

Muddle (i.e., mash together) the sugar, bitters, soda, and the orange wedge until the sugar is dissolved. Then add ice and whiskey. Stir and garnish with a cherry. Serve in a rocks glass.

Orange Blossom

2 ounces gin
Orange juice

Put three ice cubes into a highball glass. Pour in gin. Fill the glass with orange juice, stir, and serve.

Piña Colada

6 ounces rum
8 ounces cream of coconut or coconut milk
8 ounces pineapple juice
Ice

Combine rum, cream of coconut, and pineapple juice in a blender. Blend at low speed to mix the ingredients. Fill a blender with ice, and blend on high speed until the ice is grainy. Serve in a Collins glass.

Rum and Coke

2 ounces rum
Coke

Put three ice cubes into a highball glass. Pour in the rum. Fill the glass with Coke, stir, and serve.

7 and 7

1 part Seagram's Seven Canadian whiskey
1 part 7-Up

Mix with ice and serve in a highball glass.

Screwdriver

2 ounces vodka
Orange juice

Put three ice cubes into a highball glass. Pour in the vodka. Fill the glass with orange juice, stir, and serve.

Sea Breeze

1½ ounce vodka
2 ounces grapefruit juice
2 ounces cranberry juice

Shake all ingredients with ice and strain into a highball glass over ice cubes.

Sex on the Beach

1 ounce vodka
½ ounce peach schnapps
Orange juice
Grenadine (optional)

Measure one ounce of vodka and a half-ounce of peach schnapps. Pour into a highball glass over ice. Fill the rest with orange juice and add a dash of grenadine. This can also be consumed as a shooter.

Singapore Sling

½ ounce grenadine
1 ounce gin
2 ounces sweet and sour mix
Carbonated water
½ ounce cherry brandy
Cherry

Pour grenadine, gin, and the sweet and sour mix into a Collins glass over ice cubes and stir well. Fill with carbonated water and top with cherry brandy. Add the cherry and serve in a highball glass.

Tequila Sunrise

4 ounces tequila
Orange juice
½ ounce grenadine

Pour tequila into a highball glass and top with orange juice. Stir. Add grenadine by tilting the glass and pouring the grenadine down the inside of the glass. The grenadine should go straight to the bottom and then rise up slowly through the drink.

Tom Collins

2 ounces gin
1 ounce lemon juice
1 teaspoon sugar
3 ounces club soda
Cherry
Orange wedge

In a shaker half-filled with ice cubes, combine the gin, lemon juice, and sugar. Shake well. Strain into a Collins glass about half-full with ice. Top off with club soda, then stir and garnish with the cherry and an orange slice.

Vodka or Gin Chiller

2 ounces vodka or gin
Ginger ale

Put three ice cubes into a highball glass. Pour in vodka or gin. Fill the glass with ginger ale, stir, and serve.

Whiskey Sour

2 ounces bourbon, rye, or Canadian whiskey
1 ounce sour mix
Maraschino cherry
1 orange slice

Pour the whiskey and the sour mix into a shaker with ice. Shake vigorously. Strain over ice in a rocks glass and garnish with a maraschino cherry and an orange slice.

White Russian

1½ ounce vodka
½ ounce Kahlúa
Cream or milk to fill

Stir ingredients with ice and strain into a rocks glass with ice.

Zombie

1 ounce light rum
½ ounce creme de almond
1½ ounce sweet and sour mix

½ ounce Triple Sec
1½ ounce orange juice
½ ounce 151-proof rum

Shake all ingredients (except the 151-proof rum) with ice and strain into a Collins glass over ice cubes. Float the 151 on top by pouring slowly over a teaspoon, bottom turned up, and serve.

38

Drinking Games

Years ago, I went to a Christmas party with a college friend named Mark. We were on fall break and he invited me to go to this party his stepmother was throwing for some of her real estate associates because he didn't have a date and so we could get drunk and rag on people together. At the time, I wasn't in party mode, but I went because Mark is just one of those guys that every time you go out together you either end up in jail or have the best time of your life.

The party started out as expected, dull and boring, and I had to talk to people I didn't know, or didn't really care to know. At the time, the only saving grace was that the bar was stocked with premium liquor, and I didn't have to drive anywhere that night. About an hour into the party, Mark and I were a little buzzed, and very bored. We were in the kitchen with a handful of other guests when I saw Mark's eyes light up. He decided that now would be a great time to play a drinking game. Since I thought it would be funny, and I wanted to see what Mark's stepmom would do to him, I agreed. The game started with just me, Mark, and a guy we didn't know.

We started to play Actor and Movie (see below), and within fifteen minutes, we had about ten new players. Everyone from the wife of the president of the company to the boyfriend of the receptionist was playing. I thought Mark's stepmom was going to kill us when she found out what we were doing, but to my surprise, she just rolled her eyes at us and left the room. As it turned out, she was happy that everyone was having a good time. Although it may not be a great idea to organize a friendly game of quarters at your next company Christmas party, you may want to keep the thought in the back of your mind if you are ever at a party in desperate need of some fun. Drinking games have tremendous "party turn-around power."

Actor and Movie

Rules: A person names an actor or actress. You then go around to each of the other players who must name a movie that the actor or actress was in. It keeps going until someone can't think of one or there are no movies left. If a player can't think of one they take one drink, and also drink for every movie that the other players can think of in 60 seconds. When it is your turn to think of a movie there is a 30-second time limit. Teams are allowed, but if a team gets stuck, and the other players can think of five different movies the whole team has to drink.

I Never

Rules: The game starts by someone saying "I never [did whatever]." It is more fun if you try to be creative. If you have done what the person says that they have never done, then you must drink. If someone doesn't drink for something that someone else knows that they have done they must finish their drink.

Quarters

Rules: Quarters can be played with any number of players, but it is best played with three to six participants. Competitors sit around a hardwood or hard-surfaced table. To decide who goes first, spin the quarter and when it stops it will be pointing at the person who will go first. Whoever the eagle's beak or Washington's nose is pointing at will go first. The shooter tries to bounce the quarter off the table and into a glass. If the quarter goes into the glass the shooter chooses a person at the table to drink. If the quarter misses the glass then the shooter has to drink. The amount of each drink should be determined prior to beginning the game. The shooter's turn is over when he or she does not make the quarter into the cup after two tries. Play then proceeds to the next shooter. To make things interesting the shooter can make new rules after making three quarters into the glass in a row. If any rules are broken, the guilty party must consume.

Drug Dealer

Rules: Get as many playing cards as there are players. There should be one Ace and one King mixed in the cards. Mix up the cards and distribute one to each player. The player with the Ace is the drug dealer and the person with the King is the cop. The drug dealer must wink at the other players, and any player who sees that wink must say, "The deal has been made." After the deal has been made the cop must identify himself and it is up to him to determine who the dealer is. For every wrong guess the cop must drink for 5 seconds. If the cop sees the wink, he must drink for 5 seconds. This game is best played with a large group of people. Players may also bluff and pretend that they have seen the wink when they actually have not.

Asshole

Rules: The first hand is used to determine everyone's rank for the next hand. Deal out all the cards, start with the person to the left of the dealer and move in a clockwise direction. The object of the game is to get rid of all of your cards. If you are starting, you can lay down any card or cards, the only thing is that the person following you must lay down a card or cards of equal or greater value. If no one can lay anything down, then the table is clear, and the same person goes again. (For example, if a player lays down two Jacks, the next person must lay down either two Jacks or higher to stay in play.) Anyone who can't lay down cards must drink for 5 seconds. Also, if a person lays down the same card or cards as the previous player then the next player is skipped and that person must drink for 5 seconds.

Play continues until all the cards have been played. After the first hand there is a ranking system that is as follows: President, Vice President, Secretary, Asshole. (If you are playing with more than four people then add new cabinet members.) Whoever goes out first becomes the new president for the next game, the second becomes the vice president, and so on. For the following rounds, the same rules apply but in addition anyone who ranks above you can tell you to drink at any time.

The asshole must always deal the cards and clear the cards. The asshole must always give his two best cards to the president, and the president gives his two worst cards to the asshole. If the president stays in office for more than three consecutive rounds he can begin to make rules. For example, no one can say the word *drink.* Offenders must drink for 5 seconds.

39

How to Cure Hiccups

Hiccups are spasms of the diaphragm that are caused when the diaphragm is out of synch. Hiccups occur fairly often when one drinks alcohol. They can be embarrassing, not to mention incriminating if a cop stops you. The following are some of the more popular cures for hiccups. Use whatever works best for you.

1. Drink a large glass of water.
2. Drink a large glass of water with a teaspoon of sugar dissolved in it.
3. French kiss your girlfriend or wife.
4. Take a slice of lemon and put three to five dashes of Angostura bitters on it. Chew the lemon pulp and swallow the bitters and lemon juice. Discard the lemon rind. (Some people like to put a little sugar on the lemon to sweeten the taste of the bitters and sour lemon.)

The only sure-fire cure is number 4; it has worked for me and other bartenders every time. Numbers 1 and 2 work for some people, some of the time. Number 3 works about half the time but is twice the fun of all the others put together!

40

How to Prevent or Cure a Hangover

The August of my twenty-first year I decided I was going to move in with one of my friends. Paul's roommate had moved out, and I really didn't feel comfortable bringing girls back to my mother's basement anymore.

The day I moved in, which was a Friday afternoon, Paul was going out of town with his girlfriend. It was about six o'clock, he said good-bye, and since August in Virginia is very hot and unbelievably humid, he said I could feel free to watch TV in his room while he was gone. (Paul had a huge TV and a window air-conditioning unit. I had neither.) He also said in passing that he had just purchased a new carpet and to be careful not to spill anything on it. I assured him that I would be careful as he was walking out the door. Do you see where this story is heading? Also, did I mention that Paul is about 6 foot 4 inches and at that time he had arms the size of oak trees?

That Saturday night I went to some Jimmy Buffet theme party with a few friends where there was a trash can full of some alcohol-laced Kool-Aid they were trying to pass off as some exotic tropical drink. I didn't care what it was, just as long as it was free. The last thing I remember was that I was having a chugging contest with a skinny guy named Mark because we figured out that we lived two apartments down from each other and we both thought that Terry Bradshaw and the Pittsburgh Steelers were the shit.

I woke up the next morning in Paul's room, with both the air-conditioner and the TV on full blast. I was fully clothed, except that I was missing my right shoe. (I found it later that day in the kitchen—I never solved that mystery.) I slowly moved to get off the couch and put my feet on the floor. That's the only time I have not been able to get to the bathroom to throw up.

Not only had I puked on Paul's new carpet, I had puked a lot and it was blue from the Kool-Aid. Even though I knew I was screwed and Paul was going to kill me, I did not care. I did not care, because I have never been so hung over in my life. It was one of those "two full days to recover and I will never do that again" hangovers. Needless to say, I didn't learn my lesson, and I also had to buy Paul a new rug so he wouldn't kill me.

Hangover Prevention

1. Eat before you drink. Food slows down the absorption of alcohol as well as protects the stomach.
2. Stick to one type of drink if you can, and don't mix grapes (wine) and grains (beer and bourbon). Drinking carbonated alcoholic beverages on top of straight alcoholic beverages just supercharges the alcohol into your bloodstream, getting you *very* drunk.
3. Try not to smoke as much. Smoking makes you want to drink more. Alcohol makes your veins expand and nicotine makes them contract. (This is why they go hand in hand.)
4. Drink *a lot* of water before you got to bed. Alcohol dehydrates your brain and makes it shrink. Close your eyes and imagine your brain shrinking. I'm sure you can understand why this causes it to hurt.

As prevention goes, I'm sorry to say that's about it. If you are going to go all out and get hammered, then you must also be prepared to suffer the consequences.

Hangover Cures

The main causes of a hangover are dehydration and vitamin and mineral depletion. Sometimes, alcohol withdrawal also has something to do with it. Often, just drinking water will *not* rehydrate your body. This is because the electrolyte balance in your bloodstream is out of whack due to the depletion of minerals by the alcohol. Sodium and potassium are the two minerals that put the electrolytes back into balance. Certain sports drinks like Gatorade contain electrolytes as does Pedialyte, a drink given to babies when they get dehydrated. The sugar in the Gatorade will also help, but if your stomach is queasy and you can't stand the thought of drinking something sweet, try the Pedialyte, it doesn't contain the sweeteners found in sports drinks. Salt and potassium supplements washed down with lots of water also work.

Unlike hangover prevention, everyone swears that they have the best hangover cure. I have compiled some of the most popular cures, but the best advice I can give is stick with what works best for you.

If I Were a Doctor I Would Say:

1. Drink a lot of water or an electrolyte solution to rehydrate your body.
2. Take an analgesic like ibuprophen (Advil) or naproxen sodium (Aleve) for your headache, if they don't bother your stomach. Always take them with food, since taking medicine on an irritated empty stomach is just asking for more pain. Aspirin is *not* recommended since it can really irritate your stomach and *never take acetaminophen* (Tylenol) since acetaminophen combined with alcohol can cause *liver damage.* Headache powders contain aspirin, so only use these if you have a strong stomach.
3. Take vitamin and mineral supplements. A couple of good multivitamins should do the trick. Specifically, you need to replenish your B vitamins, vitamin C, and zinc. Vitamins A and E will also help. They work best when taken along with food.
4. Eat a well-balanced breakfast or brunch. Alcohol will raise your insulin levels and make you feel weak and worn out. Eating will counteract this side effect and raise the glucose levels in your bloodstream. If your stomach is too upset to eat solid food, drink some Gatorade; it will put sugar in your bloodstream as well as balance your electrolyte levels.
5. *After* you have rehydrated your body, you can do some moderate exercise to break a sweat. Sweating helps eliminate the toxins left over from the alcohol. Make sure to drink plenty of sports drinks or water while you exercise; otherwise you will faint from overheating.

If I Were a Bartender I Would Say:

1. Blend 7 oz. carrot juice, 1 oz. beet juice, 3 oz. celery juice, and ½ oz. of parsley juice. Try not to puke when drinking it.
2. Drink a lot of cranberry juice, and take a hot shower.

3. Go to a 7-Eleven and get an extra-large Gatorade, two BC headache powders, and wash it all down with any form of fast food. Taco Bell has been know to work best.
4. Drink gingerale mixed with Angostura bitters.
5. Drink a teaspoon of lime juice and a pinch of cumin mixed in a cup of orange juice.
6. Drink 4 oz. water, the juice of half a lemon, and a few drops of fennel oil.
7. Drink tomato juice and black coffee, with two raw eggs, an analgesic, vitamin B and vitamin E.
8. Drink a Bloody Mary for the vodka.
9. Drink another beer. (Sometimes food, water, vitamins, Gatorade, minerals, etc. are just not enough. Your body is experiencing alcohol withdrawal and needs another drink. Try to limit your intake to one or two drinks because if you do this too often you'll wind up in the Betty Ford clinic!)

PART FIVE

Baby, You Can Drive My Car:
A Crash Course in Automotive Basics

41

How to Change a Car Battery

When I was eighteen and moved out of my parents' house and into an apartment I had two roommates. One of my roommates, who, for the purpose of not causing him too much embarrassment, I will refer to as "Sam," was the inspiration for the inclusion of this subject in this book. You see, one day Sam came home with a truck that he had just purchased for $450. It was a pumpkin orange 1963 International Scout and, even though it was in pretty rough shape, it was a cool truck. A real man's truck that came complete with bald tires, a cracked windshield, and numerous rust holes in the body. I think it ran for about a week before it started having problems.

The first thing to go wrong was that it wouldn't start in the mornings when it was cold outside, and based upon some conversations Sam had with an auto mechanic, he came to the conclusion that it would be in his best interest to purchase a new and stronger battery. Now, I am sure that a vast majority of you are not familiar with the electrical system of a 1963 International Scout, but if you are, then I am sure you know that it is not the best ever made. When Sam installed the new battery, he accidentally installed it *backwards,* and due to the lack of an adequate fuse box that would accommodate a stronger battery, it resulted in a completely fried electrical system. The cost for repair was estimated at about $800 more than he paid for the truck. I think Sam sold it for about $200 a few days later to the same mechanic who gave him the estimate.

Changing a car battery is something that all men are expected to know, and as a result of this expectation, men will always be too embarrassed to ask for help if we are not sure of how to do it correctly. This is dedicated to all of those men.

Before We Begin: What Is a Car Battery?

Car batteries are commonly known as lead-acid batteries or wet-cell batteries. These batteries weigh about 30 pounds, contain about eighteen pounds of lead, which is a toxic metal, and about one gallon of sulfuric acid, a corrosive liquid. These two components are contained in a corrosion and heat-resistant housing made of plastic. The primary function of a lead-acid battery is to generate a high electric charge that is needed to start a car; it is considered "dead" if it can no longer hold enough charge to start a car.

If batteries are not disposed of properly, they can be extremely harmful to the environment. As a result, many states have passed laws against the illegal dumping and disposal of these batteries. When a lead-acid battery is illegally dumped, it can corrode and release lead and lead-contaminated sulfuric acid into the environment. This can pollute drinking water sources such as lakes, rivers, streams, and groundwater. If lead-acid batteries are burned in incinerators, lead can remain in the ash and be released into the air. An estimated 138,000 tons, or 65 percent, of the lead found in our contaminated water comes from lead-acid batteries. Many scrap-metal dealers, service stations, and lead smelters will accept dead lead-acid batteries for recycling. About 90 percent of all car batteries are recycled today, and a majority of automotive stores will not let you purchase a new battery until you have turned in an old one.

Changing a Car Battery

In most cars the battery is usually located under the hood of the car, either on the front left or front right side. (The reason I say *usually* is because the battery in my brother's 1979 VW Bug was located under the back seat.) The battery is held in place by a bracket, which is held down by a bolt or couple of bolts. After removing the bolts and the bracket the only thing left holding the battery in place is the connection cables.

In modern batteries, as you face the battery, the *positive* terminal will be on the *right* side, and the *negative* terminal will be on the *left* side. If you think you will have difficulty remembering this, then it may be in your best interest to label the cables connected to the terminals with masking tape. The positive battery terminal should be marked with "+" sign and be colored red, while the negative terminal should be marked with a "–" sign and be colored black. The cables may also be marked in the same way. As you may have guessed, red just so happens to be the universal sign for positive or "hot," and black is the sign for negative or "cold."

The cables are attached to the terminals by terminal posts, usually hexheaded bolts. Find the proper-sized wrench and loosen the bolts in a counterclockwise direction. Take off the *negative cable first*, then the positive. Remove the posts (bolts) and put them in a cup or somewhere safe where they can't roll away on you. Pull the cables away from the battery and lift out the old battery.

Check to see that the cable connectors are free of corrosion. Sometimes, acid from the battery will corrode the ends of the cable. Use a solution of baking soda and water to neutralize the acid and scrub the solution onto the cable connectors and terminal-post bolts with a wire brush. Auto parts stores sell inexpensive cone-shaped wire brushes to go inside the connectors or you can use rough steel wool. Make sure that new bare metal is all that touches the terminals of the new battery. Corroded or even just oxidized cable connectors will require more output from the battery to overcome electrical resistance due to oxidation or corrosion. Severely corroded cable connectors must be replaced. It's also a good idea to clean off the clamp-down bolts, clamps, and holding tray with the baking soda solution.

Replace the old battery with a new battery of the same size (a larger size may not fit in your tray, while a smaller size may not clamp down tightly enough), type (low-maintenance or maintenance-free), cold-cranking amps capacity (CCA rating), and reserve capacity (RC rating). All this information is on the old battery. Before connecting the cable connectors to the battery terminals, thinly coat the terminals and connectors with Vaseline or some other high temperature grease. This will help prevent corrosion. Clamp the battery down with the bracket and reconnect the cables in *reverse order*, i.e., connect the *positive* (red "+") connector to the positive terminal *first*, then attach the negative (black "–") connector to the negative terminal. Don't over-tighten the battery-post terminals (i.e., the hex-headed bolts) because you can crack the plastic case and cause acid to leak all over—not what you want.

In case you're wondering what would happen if you put the positive cable on the negative terminal and vice-versa, just remember what happened to Sam. By the way, Sam was lucky, instead of just shorting out the whole electrical system (which can include your car's computer, radio/tape/CD system, lights, etc.) the wrongly connected battery also could have exploded like an acid-filled bomb. Don't even *think* about doing it, and make doubly sure that the positive connector is connected to the positive terminal and the negative connector to the negative terminal. It's not hard, just look to be sure.

42

How to Jump-Start a Car

Jump-starting your car is a piece of cake, unless you don't keep jumper cables in your car. Batteries usually go dead for two reasons: Its life span is over and will not hold a charge anymore or you leave your lights on. If your battery will not keep a charge, and you try to jump-start your car in hopes of recharging the battery, it will only go dead again within about 12 hours. This is the reason why it is important to keep jumper cables in your car at all times.

What You Will Need

1. Jumper cables
2. Another car with a good battery

Step 1. Find a person with a car that has a good battery and who has agreed to help. Open the hoods of both cars and find out which side of the car the battery is on. The car with the good battery we will call the "live" car. Your car with the dead battery will be the "dead" car.

Step 2. Drive the "live" car close enough to the "dead" car so that the jumper cables will reach from one battery to the other.

Step 3. Check the owner's manual for both vehicles before you try to jump-start the car. Some manufacturers (although very few) recommend that the "live" car should *not* be running during a jump-start, then again, starting the "dead" car with the "live" car running will prevent both cars from being disabled. Check the manufacturer's procedure in the manual to avoid any hassle. If it is below 8–10 degrees Fahrenheit, make sure the battery isn't *frozen*. If it is, thaw the battery *first*. Turn off any unnecessary electrical accessories and lights on both cars and put them in park with the emergency brake on. Start the "live" car and make sure it has run for 2–3 minutes at a fast idle to fully charge its battery.

Step 4. On the jumper cables start with the *red* clips, which are for the positive terminals on your battery. Positive terminals have a "+" sign on them, and also may have a red rubber cover that needs to be pulled back. Attach the red clips to the metal positive terminal of the "dead" car's battery and then to the battery of the "live" car, *being very careful not to let the other clips touch each other. Never touch metal to the positive end of jumper cables.* This will cause sparks to fly and may short out the "live" battery.

Step 5. Attach the *black* clip of the jumper cables to the "live" car's negative ("−") terminal.

Step 6. Now connect the last black unattached clip to the frame on the "dead" car or to something grounded *away from the battery*. The negative clip will be grounded if it is attached to either any exposed (i.e., unpainted) metal on the "dead" car's engine or on the "dead" car's frame.

Step 7. Let the "live" car run for 5 minutes at a high idle.

Step 8. If the manufacturer recommends it, turn off the "live" car. If not, keep it running at a high idle. Try to start the "dead" car. If nothing happens, make sure all the cables are connected properly. Next rev the "live" car's engine a little. Let it run for a few minutes at a high idle, and try again. It may take up to 10 minutes. If your "dead" car still doesn't start, call a tow truck, the problem may be the starter motor or the alternator.

Step 9. If your car starts, keep it running for several minutes at a high idle, and turn off the "live" car.

Step 10. Disconnect the black (negative "–")cables first, and *make sure not to touch the cables to each other.* Then disconnect the red (positive "+") cables.

Step 11. Drive away and go directly to a service station to have your electrical system checked. Don't be an idiot and go to the store and turn off your car. Your battery may not have had enough time to recharge, or it could be totally dead, or something other than the battery may need repair.

43

How to Change Your Oil

Learning to change your oil is a rite of passage and more or less a time for father and son bonding. My father taught me how to change the oil in my car, just as his father taught him. It is a simple job that can be easily and inexpensively done. Unfortunately, it is a very messy job, and the mess can't be avoided so wear old clothes. I think everyone should know how to change the oil in a car and experience changing it a few times in your life. However, after performing the task a half-dozen times or so, it is time to graduate to the next level. The next level is paying someone else to do it.

What You Will Need

1. Four to five quarts of new motor oil. (If you have no clue as to what type, consult your owner's manual or an auto parts store can tell you.) At the end of the chapter there is an explanation.
2. A new oil filter. An auto parts store can help you with this also; just tell them the make, model, and year of your car.
3. You'll need an oil filter wrench to remove the old filter, and a wrench to fit your car's oil drain plug. Use a socket or box wrench of the appropriate size to avoid stripping the plug.

4. An oil-changing pan. (A short pan to fit under the car. Make sure it can hold four to five quarts.)
5. A funnel.

Safety Tips

1. Check your owner's manual for specific safety measures during an oil change.
2. Place blocks against the rear wheels to prevent the car from rolling.
3. *Never* use a car "tire" jack to lift the car to change your oil.
4. Don't permit anyone inside the car while you are changing the oil.
5. Be careful of the oil that is draining. It can be extremely hot.
6. Avoid prolonged skin contact with motor oil.
7. Remove motor oil from your skin by washing thoroughly with grease-cutting soap and water. (Simple Green or Goop are examples of good grease-cutting soaps.)
8. Don't use gasoline, thinners, or other solvents to remove oil from your skin.

Step 1. Using either a hydraulic jack or automotive ramps, position the car in a driveway so that the front end is about a foot off the ground. (Never *ever* use the jack that is in the trunk that was put there for changing flat tires. It is not designed for this type of use.) If you don't have a hydraulic jack or ramps, park the car on a level piece of ground but make sure there is enough clearance under the car so you can reach the oil pan and oil filter. Let the engine run for 5 minutes, then turn the engine off. This lets the engine oil heat up a little so that it all drains when the plug is taken out.

Step 2. Move the drain pan so that it is positioned under the oil pan's drain plug. (Note: The drain plug is located on the actual oil pan. The oil pan is the lowest part of the engine under the car. Check your owner's manual.) Loosen the drain plug with a wrench, but make the last few turns by hand (caution: don't burn your hands on the draining hot oil) so the plug does not fall into the oil pan. (It is not fun fishing for a drain plug in a pan of hot oil, which is like some medieval torture ritual.) Clean the plug with a rag so it is ready for replacement.

Step 3. Place the drain pan under the car, beneath the *oil filter.* Remove the old filter with the filter wrench in a *counterclockwise* motion, and let the oil from the old filter drain into the pan. Depending on the make and model of the car, you may have to get under the car to get to the oil filter. Whatever you do, be very careful.

Step 4. After the engine has drained fully, replace and fully tighten the oil drain plug, but don't tighten it so hard that you strip the head. Prior to installing the new oil filter, put some clean oil on your fingertip and rub it on the oil filter's seal. (The seal is a black rubber ring surrounding the opening where you screw the oil filter back on to the engine.) This will assure a leak-free fit when the new filter is installed. Put a little clean oil on the threads of the filter as well. Tighten the new filter as tight as you can *by hand.* Then use the filter wrench and give it a *half-turn,* no more, in a *clockwise* direction.

Step 5. Check the owner's manual to see how much oil the engine takes, it is usually four to five quarts. At the top of the engine you will find the oil cap (often it has the word *oil* written on it; if you can't find it, look in your owner's manual for its location). Unscrew the cap, add the new oil, and check the oil pan's drain plug and filter to make sure they are properly sealed. Remove the car from the ramps or the jack. Prior to driving, run the engine for a few minutes to circulate the new oil into the filter and engine. Check the filter and drain plug for leaks. If there are any leaks shut off the car, tighten the plug or filter where the leaking occurred, restart the car and check again until there are no leaks.

What to Do With the Used Oil

1. Collect the used oil in a disposable container or specially designed oil drain container. Old Coke two-litre bottles work well.
2. Take the container of used oil to a collection center. A gas station with a garage can accept it, if not, they can tell you where to take it.

Whatever You Do *Do Not*

1. Throw used oil on the ground.
2. Throw used oil in the trash.
3. Spread used oil on roads. (Yes, some idiots have actually done this.)
4. Pour used oil into sewer or storm drains.

If I find out that you have disposed of your oil in any one of the above ways, especially number 3, I will hunt you down and kill you. But seriously folks, oil contamination is one of the leading sources of groundwater pollution and can lead to cancer and other horrible consequences and it's just as easy to dump it at your local auto parts store or garage.

What Do the Numbers and Grades of Oil Mean?

To tell you how thick or thin an oil is, the Society of Automotive Engineers (SAE) has established a viscosity classification that appears on the top of oil cans and the labels of plastic bottles. The numbers that appear on today's oil labels are actually a combination of two different oil classifications.

The numbers you see on oil cans that generally go from 5W (which would be for very thin oil used in extremely cold weather) up to 50 (which would be for very thick oils that have special uses like racing engines), are the numbers designated by the Society of Automotive Engineers. The "W" classification (for *winter*) basically gives an indication of how low the outdoor temperature can get before the oil stops providing good engine starting capabilities. The lower the number, the thinner the oil, which is needed at low temperatures. Six "W" grades are specified by SAE, these are 0W, 5W, 10W, 15W, 20W, and 25W.

The other classification is the "non-W" SAE grades and are marked by a viscosity measured at 100°C (210°F). This is done to tell the user how thick or thin the oil will be at engine operating temperatures. There are 5 "non-W" SAE Grades 20, 30, 40, 50 and 60. Again, the smallest numbers are the thinnest in viscosity.

Years ago, a person who had a car and lived in a cold climate would change to low viscosity such as 5W (or 20) oil in the winter, and then to a higher viscosity such as 15W (or 30) for summer driving. Nowadays, there are multi-grade oils such as 5W-30 or 10W-40 that can start an engine in cold temperatures but provide higher grade viscosity at maximum operating temperatures.

A lot of people have confused the two rating systems and think that they are one number. They think the oil classification is 10W-30, when it is in reality two classifications on two different scales: 10W and 30 not 10W-30. Hey, you learn something new every day!

44

How to Change a Flat Tire

The first thing you need to do prior to getting a flat tire is to check your spare. Every so often it is a good idea to check your spare tire to make sure:

1. That it's actually there
2. That it's properly inflated
3. That you know what it looks like (most spare tires are smaller than standard sized tires and are known as doughnuts)
4. That all the parts to the jack are there. (If you have purchased a used car, especially an old one, it is possible that the jack has been removed or parts are missing.)

I know that checking your spare tire may not be a "cool" thing to do, but it is a lot cooler than being stranded out in the middle of nowhere, with a flat tire, and a flat spare or no jack.

Step 1. Control the Car Pull Over

There are two basic types of flat tires. The first is called a blowout. A blowout happens when the tire explodes and loses air very rapidly. They are usually caused by sudden and severe damage to the tire (like running over a sharp object in the road). Blowouts are characterized by a loud noise (that would be the tire popping), and then your car will pull toward the side of the car with the blown tire. Try to remain calm, and keep the car under control by backing off the accelerator and slowly braking to a halt (do not stomp on the brake!). The second type of flat tire is known as a slow leak. Slow leaks are usually caused by a puncture, such as running over a nail. Your car will become sluggish and harder to drive. It is usually not hard to tell if you have a flat tire or are getting a flat. Your car will drive much differently.

In either case, the first thing you have to do is to pull off the road as soon as possible. Look for the flattest, straightest area that is out of the way of traffic. Don't drive for miles looking for the best place to pull off, this will cause severe damage to your car, as well as your tire rim. (Having to replace a tire *and* a rim can be very expensive.) Pull off at the first safe area you come to and turn on your hazard lights.

Step 2. Get the Spare and the Jack

After pulling off the side of the road, and inspecting the damage, you will need to get the spare tire and the jack out of the car. It is usually located in the trunk, either under the floor board and carpet, or mounted up against the side of the car on the inside of the trunk. If you can't find it for some reason, check your owner's manual. First, remove the spare tire, and all the parts of the jack. In many cases there will be two or three pieces to the jack, and the jack handle will usually double as the lug-nut remover. Check the jack handle prior to tearing apart the trunk of your car swearing the lug nut wrench is not there. Put blocks behind the wheels to prevent the car from moving when you jack it up.

Step 3. Removing the Lug Nuts

Some cars have hubcaps that cover the lug nuts. To get the hubcap off, use the flat end of the jack handle. (It will be flat and look like a large screwdriver.) Insert it into the slot at the edge of the cover, or the end of the actual hubcap, and pry it open. Once the hubcap is removed, you have to remove the lug nuts. Hopefully you will read this before actually getting a flat tire, because if you jack up your car prior to loosening the nuts, the tire will spin as you try to get it off. Believe me, it is very annoying to jack the car off the ground and realize you have to start over. Put the lug wrench (this could be the end of the jack handle or a cross-shaped tool with sockets and a hubcap remover, it depends on the car) on the lug nuts (there are usually four or five) and turn *counterclockwise*. If you have trouble loosening the nuts, first try some penetrating oil or WD-40 on the threads and nuts. If that doesn't work, place your foot on the end of the lug wrench, while holding onto the car, and step onto it with your full weight. If it still doesn't loosen up try bouncing up and down. If that doesn't work try pounding on the handle with a rock. What ever you have to resort to, be careful. When you loosen all of the lug nuts it is time to jack up the car. *Don't try to take the lug nuts all the way off the car, you only have to loosen them at this point.*

Step 4. Jacking Up the Car

The first thing you have to do is find the place on the car that is designated for placement of the jack so it is possible to actually raise the car off the ground. Check your owner's manual. Most modern cars have four reinforced places where their jacks are to be placed. If you have a flat tire in the front of the car, place the jack on the frame about 8 inches *behind* the front wheel. (On the frame of the car, not in the wheel well.) In many cases, if you look behind the front tires there will be a notch in the frame where the jack is to be placed. The same goes for the rear tires. There is a reinforced part of the frame, *in front* of the rear tire. (Not on the bumper.) These spots on the car have been reinforced to hold the weight of the car. Once you have located those spots, brush away pebbles and other obstructions and make sure you correctly position the jack so it is flat on the ground. Turn, crank, or jack the handle until the car and tire are off the ground. Remember you have to get a fully inflated tire on to the tire mount, so make sure you have jacked the car far enough off the ground.

Step 5. Changing the Wheel

Once the flat tire is off the ground you can now remove the lug nuts. I recommend removing the bottom lug nuts first. As you will see, as the lug nuts are removed, the tire may begin to pull away from the car. It is better to have the tire pull up (the bottom of the tire will begin to move toward you as the bottom nuts are removed) than to have it pull down and fall off on top of you. (If you remove the top nuts first.) If the tire is not loose then you may have to pull or bang on it to get it free. Be careful as it comes loose, you don't want to ruin a good shirt by being knocked over by a heavy tire. Once you have the flat off, it is time to put on the spare.

Step 6. On With the Spare

Line up the holes of the spare tire with the bolts that the lug nuts attach to. As you are putting it on you may have to work it back and forth to get it mounted properly. Once you have the spare on, it is time to put the lug nuts back on. Tighten them with your hand until the wheel is held in place by the nuts, but don't tighten them all the way at this point. Now lower the jack so that the wheel is *resting* on the ground; however, don't let the full weight of the car rest on the tire because the weight can shift and make it difficult to fully tighten the lug nuts—or in a worst case scenario, strip part of the threads of the wheel-mount bolts. Don't tighten the lug nuts in order; tighten them opposite from each other, or in the case of an odd number, tighten them every other one until all are tightened.

Step 7. Lower the Jack and Put the Flat in the Trunk

Uncrank the jack so it is free from the car, and return the jack and the flat tire to the trunk. If you have a hubcap, don't forget to put it back on. After you have picked everything up it is time get in your car and haul ass to the appointment you've nearly missed.

If you have a full-size spare, don't forget to have the flat tire in your trunk fixed *as soon as possible*. There is always that possibility of getting another flat tire at any time. Also, if you have a small "doughnut" spare, *do not go over 55 miles per hour*. These small tires are not made for extended use, and they will blow out if driven at high speeds. Whatever the situation, get your flat tire fixed as soon as possible.

45

How to Parallel Park a Car

Parallel parking is not that hard but it is a skill that can only be mastered with practice. I have lived in the city for most of my adult life and I still have some trouble parallel parking. It takes a lot of practice, and you probably won't master it easily either. Some days are better than others, sometimes I hit the curb, or the car in front of me (oops!), or the car in back of me (oops, again!); but other times I squeeze in to the smallest of spaces so that I even amaze myself. Even though parallel parking is a learned skill, there are a few rules that will help, but only if you follow them religiously.

Step 1. Measurement

Once you have found a spot that you think will do, you have to make an eyeball measurement of the space to determine if you will have enough room to fit your car. The standard rule of thumb is at least a foot of space on each end of the car to allow enough room to maneuver. Signal with your blinkers to the doofus behind you that you intend to move either left or right.

Step 2. Positioning

Next you want to position the car about 2–3 feet away from, but parallel to, the car that is in front of the space you want to back into.

Step 3. The Initial Turn

There are two schools of thought on parallel parking. The first school is the "match the bumpers" school; the second is the "match the steering wheels" school. You can either align your car with the car in the space ahead by matching bumpers or steering wheels in parallel alignment. Try both methods and see which one works best for you. After you have positioned yourself correctly next to the car in front of the space you want to park in, it is time to back up. When you have reached proper alignment turn your wheel hard toward the curb (you can start with a revolution-and-a-half of the steering wheel). *Slowly (and I do mean slowly*, even if you have to make someone else wait) start to back up.

Step 4. Turn the Other Way

Again there are two schools of thought as to what to do next. The first school says that when the back of your driver's seat is aligned with the rear bumper of the parallel car, you should stop and reverse the wheel (i.e., away from the curb); the other school of thought says that when your car reaches an approximately 45-degree angle, you should stop and reverse the wheel. Try both methods and see which one works best for you. After you get the hang of it, you won't have to stop, but can do this in one fluid motion. Begin to back the car up again, so that the front end of the car is moving toward the curb. Be very careful to not hit the bumper of the car, both in front, and in back of the you. Once you have gotten your car into the space, pull up to make sure that you have given enough room for the car in back of you to pull out. Parallel parking is somewhat difficult (even though my directions make it sound very easy) and it will take a little time to master. If you follow my method of measuring and turning, however, you may master it in a shorter period of time.

46

How to Change a Spark Plug

The reason I decided to include how change a spark plug in this book is because spark plugs are an integral part of a combustion engine and are also a valuable tuning indicator. They can show symptoms of other problems and can reveal a lot about an engine's overall health. The reason spark plugs need to be changed is because (in layman's terms) as they grow older the sharp metal edges of the prong are rounded off and the material that makes up the electrodes is eroded away. As the edges are rounded off and electrode material is lost, the voltage required to bridge the gap between these two components increases. The ignition system must work harder to compensate for the higher voltage requirement. With the higher voltage requirement comes a greater rate of misfire and the possibility of incomplete combustion cycles. The misfires mean lower horsepower, lower fuel economy, and higher emissions (in other words, pollution). New spark plugs can restore the lost efficiency to the ignition system.

A spark plug has four basic functions.

1. It fills the hole in the top of the cylinder head
2. It acts as an insulator for the ignition system
3. It provides the spark for the combustion process
4. It removes heat from the combustion chamber

Instead of rambling on using a bunch of motor-head terms, the spark plug basically acts like a thermometer of an engine. This thermometer can be used by mechanics to determine the amount of heat in each combustion chamber, and an experienced technician can even diagnose drivability problems. Even though cars are becoming more and more complicated and computerized, changing a spark plug is one of the few maintenance jobs that you can still do at home. In our age of high technology cars, people overlook the importance of the simple spark plug.

What You Will Need

1. **New Spark Plugs.** You can get new spark plugs at your local auto parts store. Tell them the make, model, and year of your car and they will look it up in either a catalog or on a computer. They will also tell you the gap measurement and torque setting. (The number of spark plugs you will need depends on the number of cylinders your car has. A four cylinder = four spark plugs, six cylinder = six plugs, etc.)

2. **A Spark Plug Gapping Tool.** You can pick one up at an auto parts store for about a dollar.
3. **A Spark Plug Wrench or Socket.** You can get one at a hardware store, depending on what type you get, they can get expensive. Spark plug sockets are usually included in a standard socket set. You may want to borrow this one.
4. **Masking Tape.**

Step 1. Checking the Gap

The best thing to do prior to getting under the hood is to check the gap on your new plugs. Many people believe that spark plugs are pregapped at the factory, and this is true. However, this preset gap may not be right for your car. Gapping a plug is actually very easy. As you will see on a spark plug, there is a "gap" between the metal prong, and the electrode, this gap is what you will measure. After finding out what the proper gap measurement is for your car and spark plug, match it up with the setting on the spark plug gapping tool. Your spark plug is correctly gapped if the tool can slide in-between the metal and the electrode with a slight resistance. It should not be very tight, and it should not be too loose. If you are scared about the possibility of messing up your car, don't worry. My suggestion is to ask someone at an auto parts store to show you. It is very easy to learn and will take less than a minute.

Step 2. Removing the Spark Plug Wires

Every spark plug has a spark plug wire associated with it. The wires connect the spark plugs to the distributor, and must be put back in the same order. Using the masking tape, number the spark plug wires that correspond with the spark plug (Cylinder number 1 = wire number 1, etc.). In many cases the wires are different sizes so it will be hard to mess up.

Step 3. Removing the Spark Plugs

Spark plugs are tightened and loosened just like standard nuts and bolts. *Clockwise* to tighten, and *counterclockwise* to loosen. If you ever come across a spark plug that is stuck, don't try to force it out. Try working it back and forth until it comes loose or apply some lubricating oil to try to lubricate the threads. I recommend removing and installing one spark plug at a time. The reason behind this is because when you take the spark plug out of the cylinder head there is a hole that goes into the engine. It is possible for something to fall into that hole, and as a result, really screw your engine up.

Step 4. Installing New Spark Plugs

Never install new spark plugs into a hot engine. The metal in the cylinder head will expand when it is hot and the spark plugs could try to cut or "crossthread" into the metal. This will cause permanent cylinder damage, or cause the spark plug to seize in the engine. (This will make it very hard the next time you try to remove the plug.) Install and tighten new spark plugs by hand.

Step 5. Torquing the Spark Plugs

A spark plug that is improperly torqued will not be able to effectively remove heat from the cylinder head (insufficient tightening). In very severe cases the spark plug can melt, break and cause severe engine damage (excessive tightening).

As a rule of thumb after tightening your spark plugs by hand they should be tightened an additional ½–¾ of a turn for gasket-type spark plugs, and 1/16–1/8 of a turn for taper-seat spark plugs. The box the spark plugs come in will tell you which one you have. If you are unsure call your local auto parts store.

Step 6. Put Back Your Spark Plug Wires

When you are done replacing the spark plugs, replace the spark plug wires, making sure you return the same wire to the cylinder it came from. Close your hood, start your car and drive as usual. Once you change your spark plugs once, you will find that it is an easy job that can be done in a matter of minutes. Generally, any questions or concerns can be answered by either your local auto parts store or the car's owner's manual.

47

How to Drive a Stick Shift

There are a few subjects in this book that no matter what I say or how I explain cannot be substituted for the real experience, and this my friend, is one of those subjects. Driving a stick shift can only be learned through constant practice with a patient teacher.

What You Will Need

1. A car with a manual transmission
2. A patient person who is willing to teach you

3. An empty parking lot
4. A couple of hours

Why Should I Learn to Drive a Stick Shift?

There are several practical reasons to learn how to drive a stick shift, but I think that everyone should learn because driving a stick is fun. Anyway, a car with a manual transmission gets better gas mileage because you have better control of the gears when you are accelerating and driving up hills. Manual transmissions can also provide you with more control in snow and rain, and downshifting reduces wear and tear on your brakes.

Step 1. Before You Drive

Before you can actually begin to drive a car with manual transmission you have to know what to look for:

The Pedals—If you look at the floor of a car with a manual transmission you will see three pedals. The one on the far left is the clutch. The one in the middle is the brake, and the one on the far right is the gas. The clutch is used to move from one gear to another and is disengaged when it is pushed all the way to the floor.

The Stick Shift—In most cars that are not fifty years old or from a foreign country, the stick shift is located in the center of the car, between the front seats, right in front of the stereo and air conditioning controls. Cars have either four or five forward gears, neutral, and a reverse gear. Some hot rod sports cars have six gears, but I don't recommend learning how to drive a stick shift in one of these cars. Remember, you have to walk before you run. Before you actually attempt to drive a stick shift you might want to sit in a car and practice gear shifting with the car not running.

Neutral—Neutral is not a gear, but should be described as when no gear is engaged, you can press on the gas pedal and the car won't go anywhere. If you are in neutral you will be able to move the stick shift freely back and forth.

First Gear—With the clutch depressed, push the gear shift *up and to the left*.

Second Gear—With the clutch depressed, pull the gearshift *down and to the left*. This should be a fluid shift from first gear.

Third Gear—With the clutch depressed, push the gearshift *up and slightly to the right of first gear*. If the car is a five speed, the third gear will be in-between first and fifth gear.

Fourth Gear—With the clutch depressed, pull the gearshift *down and slightly to the right of second gear.* Fourth gear is in between second gear and reverse.

Fifth Gear—With the clutch depressed, push the gearshift *up and far to the right.* Fifth gear is overdrive and will only be used at speeds at or above 55 mph.

Reverse—Reverse is located below and to the right of fifth gear. In many cars you have to either push down on the shifter, or push it far to the right to engage reverse. It is set up this way to prevent you from putting your car in reverse while you are driving your car down the road at 55 mph.

Knowing When to Shift

After you get some experience under your belt, you will know by instinct when the car needs to be shifted to the next gear. Until that time you will have to make that decision based on the rpm reading on the tachometer. (rpm = revolutions per minute, tachometer = the gauge that lets you know what the rpm's are, and just so you know mph = miles per hour.)

You should shift gears as the car revs an additional 3,000 rpm or about every 15 miles an hour.

First gear 1–15 mph
Second gear 15–30 mph
Third gear 30–45 mph
Fourth gear 45–55 mph
Fifth gear 55+ mph

However, you have to remember that this is only a guideline and can vary from car to car. For example, a six-speed Corvette ZR-1 and a four-speed Hyundai will have different shifting patterns, but let's hope for the sake of the car's owner that you are learning in the Hyundai and not in a Corvette. Also, use your head; you don't have to know how to drive a stick shift to know when the car is in the right gear. If the car's engine is revving very high and making a high-pitched whining sound, then you know that it is time to shift to a higher gear. If the engine is struggling and choking then this is an indication that it is time to shift into a lower gear.

Step 2. Find a Place to Drive

Once you have suckered someone into letting you use their car to learn how to drive a stick shift, you are going to have to find a place to practice. I suggest picking a practice site such as a high school parking lot on a Saturday or Sunday afternoon. There will be plenty of space, with nothing around for you to hit.

Step 3. Practice

Once you have arrived at the parking lot, turn the car off, switch places with your teacher and get ready to begin. First, put your foot on the brake and depress the clutch all the way to the floor. (In most modern cars the car will not start unless the clutch is pressed all the way to the floor.) Make sure the car is in neutral, just to be safe, then start the car. Once the car is started, take off the parking brake (it is usually a hand brake located to the left of the driver's seat or under the left side of the dashboard; if you can't find it, ask your teacher) and put the car into first gear. Right now you will be learning the most difficult part of driving a car with a manual transmission. The trick to first gear is that you have to *let off the clutch at the same time as pressing the gas,* which I might add is not as easy as it seems. You can't release the clutch too quickly (known as *popping* the clutch), because the car will stall out (because the engine is not getting enough gas). It is also not good to rev up the engine to high rpm's and ease the clutch out slowly. This will put a lot of undue stress on the clutch, which will cause it to have to be replaced sooner than normal. (In mechanic terms this is known as *burning out* the clutch.) Before you get too excited and want to take the car out on the road, practice stopping and starting in first gear. Remember, ease the clutch out *while at the same time* pressing on the gas.

Once you have mastered first gear, the next step is to get the car going fast enough to try shifting into second and third gear. Practice first, second, and third gears until you get the hang of it. (The reason I recommend practicing only first, second, and third gears is because if you are in a parking lot you won't have enough room to get the car going fast enough to shift into fourth or fifth.)

Step 4. On the Road

After you have mastered driving in a parking lot, the next step is to actually drive on the road, and I recommend, for obvious reasons, to try to find one that doesn't have a lot of traffic. I'm sure you will find driving on an empty road similar to an empty parking lot, but once you and your teacher feel that you have gotten the hang of driving and shifting on roads, try practicing starting in first gear on a hill.

The trick when learning to start in first gear on a hill is using your parking brake. Find a hill with little traffic, stop your car, and put on the parking brake. When you are ready to go, accelerate slowly as you are releasing the clutch petal. When you feel the clutch beginning to engage (hopefully you will have had enough practice to recognize when this happens) release the parking brake. The reason you want to use the parking brake is because if you begin to stall or roll backward, you can always put on the brake and start over. Trust me, this sounds ten times easier than it looks.

Checklist

1. Put the car in first gear.
2. Let out the clutch while pressing on the gas.
3. Rev the car to about 3,000 rpm before shifting to the next gear, increasing your speed about 15 miles an hour.
4. Push the clutch in, let off the gas, and shift into second gear.
5. Let out the clutch, depress the gas, and repeat for third, fourth, and fifth gears.

What Is Downshifting?

Downshifting is the act of shifting into lower gears as you are slowing your car down. Instead of just using your brakes you can also use the gears to assist you to come to a stop. Downshifting is also very useful in bad weather. If you are driving in snow and apply your brakes, your wheels may lock up completely and you will lose control of your car. If you downshift in snow, your wheels will still be rolling, but the lower gears will help to slow down your car in a controllable manner. Downshifting basically gives you more control of the car's speed, and will also reduce any wear and tear on your brakes.

Tips

1. When driving in first gear, avoid revving the engine to high rpms and letting out the clutch slowly. This will burn out your clutch and you will have to get it replaced sooner than necessary.
2. When you are parking your car, it is best to apply the parking brake, *and* leave the car in gear. If for some reason your parking brake is loose or not properly adjusted, then the fact that your car is in gear will keep the car from rolling away.
3. Practice starting in first gear on hills in an area with little traffic.
4. When going down a steep hill, keep the car in a lower gear that will help keep the car's speed manageable. You will notice that the engine will be working harder than usual, but is should not be screeching or revving over 4,500 rpm.
5. Sometimes, a car's transmission will be more temperamental than others. You may have to push down on the gearshift or move the gearshift through a few of the other gears before the car will let you put it in reverse.

6. Never try to downshift into first gear. It is not necessary, and first gear is not designed to take the pressure of downshifting. First gear is a very low gear that is made to get the car rolling.
7. Reverse is basically first gear, but it makes the car go backward. It is designed to move the car slowly, and it is not good to drive in reverse too long or too fast. Don't try to be a comedian by driving to your friend's house in reverse. It is not good for the car.

PART SIX

A Sporting Chance:
A Crash Course in Sports and Games

48

Why I Included the Rules to Games

I am going to let you in on a little secret. I am not a huge sports fan. I don't watch ESPN's Sports Center, and I don't care how many yards Curt Warner has to throw in his next game to put you ahead five points in your fantasy football game. I consider myself an average Joe when it comes to sports. Basically, what I mean is that I do like to watch the big games, like the Superbowl or the World Series, but that is because it involves sitting around with my friends and drinking beer. To tell you the truth, in general, I really don't give a crap about sports. It's not that I am a sissy or that I never tried, but it is because I am one of those people who *royally suck* at any sport that involves having to hit, shoot, bounce, throw, drive, dribble, or putt a ball. The reason I suck at sports is because I have about 20/400 vision and my depth perception is worse than a bat (think the flying kind not the baseball kind). If I try to shoot a basketball, I miss the basket by about 10 feet. If I take a swing at a golf ball, I either completely miss or take a huge chunk out of the ground. My friends won't even let me attempt to play with their clubs anymore. You can forget about trying to hit a baseball, the last time I did that was when I was allowed to hit it off a "T" when I was eleven years old. I am not a quitter and I believe in trying, but I also believe in not embarrassing yourself and knowing your limitations.

Believe me, I wish I did like sports because it would make my life a hell of a lot easier. You see, I can't tell you how many times I have been in situations where some guy I have been introduced to, either at work or at a party, asks me about the Dallas game last week, or if I have played at this fancy-schmancy golf course across town. I only wish I could carry on a conversation and have some sort of interest. Unfortunately, you can only fake it for so long before you begin to sound like a *complete* idiot.

The following rules to sports are written for my comrades who share my feelings about sports, yet know that to survive in this dog-eat-dog world you have to have at least a working knowledge of how the games are played. However, if you are looking for information about the Power "I" formation, a discussion of the pros and cons of the designated hitter, or what a bicycle kick is, then you are looking in the wrong place. Remember, I am not writing for the sports enthusiast, but rather the person who just wants to know the fundamentals.

Please keep in mind that the rules to any particular game vary, depending on the skill level. Professional sports leagues can and usually do have different rules from college, high school, or children's leagues. The general rules of any particular game do not vary much and I will try to give the rules that apply to the game in general. The rule books for most professional sports are pretty thick and sometimes can get very arcane, but you don't need to know all the rules to enjoy the game. After all, you're just watching and having a good time, not umpiring the damned thing.

49

Baseball

What Is Baseball?

Baseball is hitting and fielding a hardball. It is played with round wooden bats and padded gloves. Baseball is played by two teams consisting of nine players each. The winner of the game is the team that scores the most runs in the allotted time period (usually nine innings). Runs are scored when a player from the batting team hits the ball and runs around all four bases. When the fielding team makes three outs, the teams switch sides and the batting team becomes the fielding team.

The Field

The field is made up of an infield and an outfield. The infield is composed of a dirt diamond that is bounded by the four bases, and the outfield is the grassy area just beyond the infield. Exact measurements of the field can vary depending upon the skill level of the team playing. Although the dimensions of the playing field may vary, in professional baseball the distance between each base is 90 feet, and the pitcher stands 60½ feet from the batter on a mound which is 10 inches high.

Officials

When a professional or semi-professional baseball game is played there usually is one chief umpire and three regular umpires. The chief umpire wears protective gear and stands behind the catcher to specifically judge whether a pitch is a strike or a ball. The chief umpire also makes any final rulings regarding any decisions made by the other three umpires. The first and third base umpires stand near their respective bases, while the second

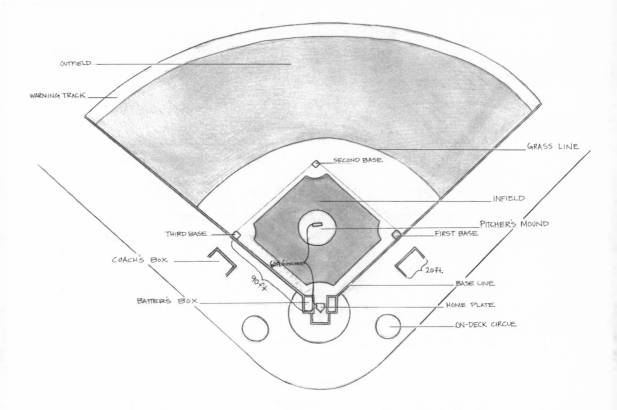

base umpire stands about 10 yards behind the first base umpire. Since the second base umpire cannot stand on the actual playing field, this position allows for the best view of what takes place at second base. The job of these officials is to judge if the batter has safely reached their respective bases. There is also an official score keeper to keep record of the game and the players' statistics.

Starting the Game

The visiting team is always up to bat for the first part of the inning. (Called the top, while the second half of the inning is called the bottom.) Before the game starts the chief umpire must receive new baseballs from the home team, and must also check the playing field and equipment to determine that it is in proper playing condition. The manager of the home team makes the decision as to if the weather conditions are good enough to start the game, but once the game has started, the chief umpire makes any decision regarding when and if the game will be stopped and restarted. No later than 5 minutes before the game is due to start the umpire must receive duplicate copies of the batting order for each team. One copy is kept for himself, and the other copy is passed on to the coach of the other team.

Next, the home team players take their defensive positions and the chief umpire yells "play ball" to start the game. (When an umpire wants to stop the play of the game he yells "time" and then yells "play ball" to resume play.) The hitting team places base coaches in the boxes right outside of first and third base. (The job of these base coaches it to tell their running players whether they should advance to the next base or not. This allows the runner to concentrate on running at top speed rather than worrying about where the ball is located.) Finally, the batter takes his position in the batting box in an attempt to hit the ball that will be pitched to him.

The Bat and Ball

The bat is basically a finished wooden stick, that cannot be more than 2¾ inches in diameter at any part and has a maximum length of 3 feet 6 inches. The ball must weigh between 5–5¼ ounces and is made of a cork or rubber center that is wrapped in yarn and covered with white cowhide. The cowhide is stitched together with bright red tightly wound yarn. Its circumference is between 9 and 9¼ inches.

Hitting the Ball

When a team is at bat each player takes his turn according to the order the coach has decided upon. Batters must stand with their feet in the batter's box and try to score runs by attempting to hit the ball that is pitched to them.

The Strike Zone

The strike zone is the area *directly* over and the same *width* as the home plate. The *height* of the strike zone is approximately between the *upper chest* (midway between the top of the shoulders and the top of the pants) of a player and the *lower thigh* (the hollow beneath the knee cap). The strike zone is individual to each player as determined by the player's stance in the batter's box and the perception of the chief umpire.

Strikes

Pitches thrown into the strike zone that are not swung at by the batter are considered strikes. If the batter swings at any ball and misses, it is considered a strike. It is also considered a strike if the batter hits the ball and it goes into foul territory and the batter has fewer than two strikes against him.

Ball

A ball is a pitch that is thrown outside of the strike zone and is not swung at by the batter. If the pitcher pitches four balls then the batter is allowed to advance to first base.

Running

A batter becomes a runner when he has either hit the ball in fair territory, has been walked to first base, the catcher interferes with him, or he has been hit by a pitch. (In professional baseball a batter can also advance to first base if the catcher drops the ball of the third pitched strike. However this is a rare call, so you may not be familiar with it. If a professional catcher can't catch the ball then he shouldn't be playing.)

Force Play

When a batter has hit the ball and is safe at first base, he is forced to advance to second base if the next batter hits a fair ball and is advancing to his position at first base. A runner is only forced to advance to the next base when he is in a position where he is forced to move by a runner behind him. (For example, if a runner is on third base and there are no other runners on second or first base, then when the next batter hits the ball and *only* advances to first base, the runner on third base is not *forced* to run.)

Stealing Bases

It is legal for runners to attempt to advance to the next base prior to the ball being hit or pitched. The only drawback is that if the ball makes it to the base prior to the runner, then that runner can be tagged out. Bases are usually stolen when the pitcher is in the final stage of his pitch and the ball is thrown toward the batter. It is also suggested that only very fast runners attempt to steal bases.

Tagging Up

When the ball is hit in the air (a fly ball), if a runner is on base, he cannot legally advance until the ball is caught. If he leaves the base prior to the ball being caught he must go back to that base and *tag up* (touch the base) before he can advance to the next base. If he has left the base prior to the ball being caught and does not get back to tag up, he can be thrown out at the base by the baseman receiving the ball from another fielder and stepping on the base. Tagging up is also called a *retouch*.

Length of the Game

A professional baseball game lasts nine innings. (Other league games may last fewer innings.) An inning has top and bottom halves and when both teams have had a chance to hit and field then an inning is complete. A half of an inning is completed when three members of the batting side are out. If the score is tied at the end of the nine innings then an additional inning is played until one team has scored more points at that inning's end. Additional innings are added until the tie is broken.

Runs

Points in baseball are called runs, and the team that has scored the most runs is the winner. A run is scored when a batter hits the ball, runs, and touches each of the four bases (first, second, third, and home). If the batter hits a fly ball and it goes over an outfield fence that is at least 250 feet from the home plate then it is considered a home run. However, before the run can officially count, he must run and touch each of the bases. (A home run can also be scored within the park if the batter is fast enough to run around all four bases before he can be tagged out.) If a batter hits the ball and it *bounces* over the outfield fence then he can only advance to second base. This is called a ground-rule double. A grand slam home run is when first, second and third bases are occupied by runners and the player that is up to bat hits a home run. A grand slam home run scores the most runs that are possible in one play. When a ball is hit into fair territory, but it is not a home run, a runner can advance, or attempt to advance, as many bases as he chooses. When a player is running, the base coach usually indicates whether to advance to the next base or to stay put. Other than home runs, the only official rule regarding the number of bases a player may attempt to take is that whenever a batter hits the ball he must at least attempt to run to first base.

Players and Substitutes

There are nine defensive players that are allowed on the field at one time. They are: the first baseman, second baseman, shortstop (positioned between second and third base), third baseman, left fielder, center fielder, right fielder, pitcher, and catcher. Substitute players can take the field at any time when the ball is out of play and as long as the chief umpire has been informed. However, when a player is substituted on the field, he is also substituted in the batting order, and once a player has been taken out of a game then he is not allowed back. The player that is substituted most often is the pitcher. Pitching the ball is a very physically demanding activity, and some pitchers become tired before the game has ended. In order to have the best possible advantage over the opposing team, the pitcher will often be replaced. It is entirely the coach's decision to substitute players.

Pitching

In professional baseball the pitcher is not allowed more than eight practice pitches after he takes the field. Once he is on the pitching mound, and the batter is in the batter's box, then he has 20 seconds to pitch the ball. A ball can only be pitched from a *set* or *wind up* position and once he has started the wind up then the pitch must be completed. Prior to winding up and pitching, the pitcher can throw the ball to any base, as long as he steps in that direction. This is often done to prevent runners from stealing bases. When a runner or runners are on base, if a pitcher stops the pitch in mid-wind up or fakes a pitch and then throws to a baseman, then this is called a *balk*. Balks are illegal and the runners on the other team are allowed to advance to the next base. A balk is also called if the pitcher does not face the base he is throwing the ball to, if he is giving an intentional base on balls, pitches the ball and the catcher is not in position, or if he makes any fake movement while on the pitching mound. It is also illegal, for obvious reasons, for the pitcher to pitch the ball directly at the batter in an attempt to injure him. The pitcher may not apply any foreign substance to the ball such as saliva, baby oil, dirt, etc. that will give him an advantage over the batter. If the pitcher is caught altering the surface of the ball then he is disqualified and thrown out of the game.

Types of Pitches

There are several different types of pitches that can be thrown in baseball. However, the two most common are the fast ball and the curve ball.

Fast Ball

A fast ball is probably the most common pitch because it places the least amount of strain on the pitcher's arm. Its name is also misleading because of the fact that it is not how hard you throw the ball, but how the ball is initially gripped and released that makes the difference. When pitching a two seam fastball your fingers line up with the seam of the baseball. When it is pitched it is a natural hand motion, with no turning or twisting of the wrist.

Curve Ball

The way a ball curves depends on the direction and the amount of spin placed on the ball. When a curve ball is pitched the ball rotates in the direction of the spin that causes the ball to curve. By controlling the direction of the spin you control the direction of the curve. Curve balls are usually gripped the same as fast balls, but the curve of the ball depends on the twist of the wrist. For example if the wrist and fingers are turned in toward the pitcher's body, the ball will curve in and down when thrown to a right-handed hitter.

Curve Ball Variations

The Slider is a curve ball that is thrown harder than a normal curve ball, and also the pitcher's wrist is turned at a 90 degree angle.

The **Screwball** is a curve ball that breaks in the opposite direction (for a right-handed pitcher the ball will curve to the right).

The **Sinker** is a curve ball that is designed to "sink" right before it gets to the batter. The batter thinks that the ball can be hit, but just at the last moment it drops below the strike zone.

Strange and Illegal Pitches

The Knuckleball—The best way a knuckleball can be described is when it is thrown it is supposed to rotate as little as possible. Without the stabilizing gyroscopic effect of the spinning, the ball becomes aerodynamically unstable and, as a result, it is harder for the batter to hit with his bat. A good knuckleball is very hard to throw.

The Spitball—A spitball is exactly what its name suggests. The pitcher would add spit, soap, Vaseline, or whatever he could find to the surface of the ball. Any additions to the ball changes the ball's aerodynamics, which makes it harder for the batter to hit. Spitballs were once legal, but were outlawed in the 1920's due to the fact that some players thought it gave the pitcher an unfair advantage. Let me put it this way, the year they were outlawed Babe Ruth hit twice as many home runs as he had the year before. You be the judge.

Outs

Batters

A batter is out: at any time the ball he has hit is caught by a fielder before it hits the ground; when the umpire calls the third strikes on the batter; if the batter tries to bunt, he already has two strikes called against him, and the ball goes over the foul line; if a runner is hit by the ball; a spectator interferes with the ball; if he interferes with a fielding player when that player is attempting to catch the ball; or if he hits a ball that can be caught in the infield with ordinary effort, there are less than two outs, and there are runners occupying first and second base. (This is called the infield fly rule.)

Runners

A runner is considered safe if he touches the base before any of the fielders touch him or the base with the ball. If the ball hits the ground prior to being caught, then the runner or the base must be touched with the ball for the runner to be tagged out. A runner is out when: a fielding player tags the runner with the ball and the runner is not in contact with a base; if a batted ball hits him when he is running between bases (yes, both players are out); if he runs more than 3 feet out of the straight line between bases (called the base line); or when a fielder tags the base prior to a forced runner reaching it.

Double Play

A double play occurs when two outs take place when the ball has been pitched once. For example, if a batter hits a ground ball and the runners are tagged out at second and first base.

Triple Play

A triple play occurs when three outs take place when the ball has been pitched once. For example, if a fly ball is caught and two forced runners are tagged out prior to them retouching their bases.

50
Basketball

What Is Basketball?

Basketball is shooting and rebounding in order to score points. It is a game played between two teams consisting of five players each. The object of the game is to score the most points in the allotted time by throwing the ball into the opposing team's basket. Other than minor adjustments in court measurements and the length of the game, basketball rules are, for the most part, the same in professional and amateur leagues.

Court and Basket

The court must be a hard surface, usually concrete or laminated wood, with a length of approximately 90 feet 22 inches and a width of 49 feet 2 inches (94 feet by 50 feet is optimal in the National Basketball Association—NBA). The basket is a metal orange ring that is 1 foot 6 inches in diameter, and there is also a white cord net that holds the ball briefly as it drops through the basket. The basket is 10 feet off the ground and is attached to a rigid backboard that measures 6 feet wide by 3 feet 6 inches high.

Officials

There are two officials on the court that are known as referees. (They are also called a referee and an umpire.) These two officials split the court between them and switch sides when there is a foul that involves a free

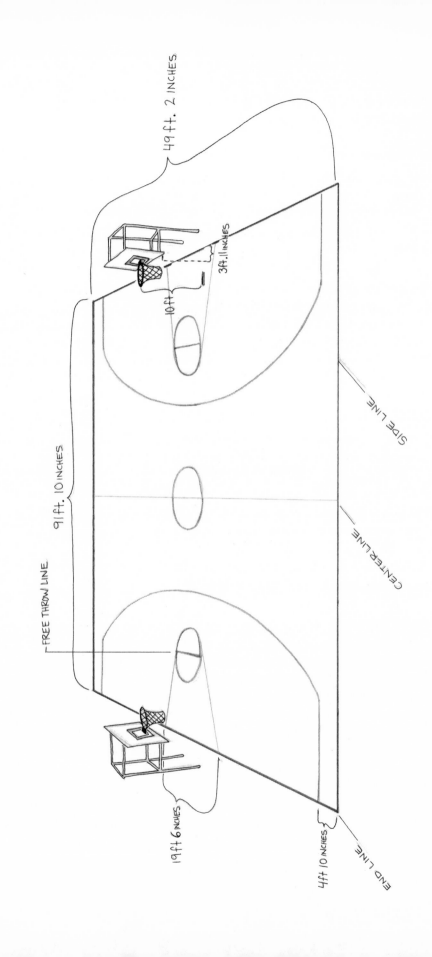

49 ft. 2 inches

3 ft. 11 inches

10 ft

91 ft. 10 inches

FREE THROW LINE

SIDE LINE

CENTERLINE

19 ft 6 inches

4 ft 10 inches

END LINE

throw or jump ball. The referees use whistles and hand signals to indicate when they have made decisions or rulings.

Forfeited Games

A game is forfeited if: a team does not have five players, the team is not on the court within 15 minutes of the game scheduled starting time, or is not on the court within 1 minute of the referee's signal. If a team forfeits a game during play then the score stands, but if it is forfeited prior to starting, the official score is 2–0.

Length

A basketball game is made up of two halves of 20 minutes each (24 minutes in the NBA). Between the halves there is a break of about 10–15 minutes. If, at the end of the second half, the score is tied, then an additional 5-minute period is added, and the teams jump ball (toss it in the air between two opposing players) for control. Five-minute periods are added until the tie is broken.

Substitutes

A player may be substituted in a game at any time when the ball is out of play. The substitute has to wait until the referee signals him to enter the court, and a time out is taken from the team if the substitute does not enter the court immediately. A player who is about to be involved in a jump ball cannot be replaced, and after a violation the offending team may make substitutions only if the other team does so first.

Playing the Game

It is customary for the visiting team to choose the basket that it wants to defend, and the teams will change sides at half time. Each team must have five players on the court, and the game starts with a jump ball.

Jump Ball

The game is started with a jump ball. A jump ball is when two players on the opposite teams stand in their respective half of the center circle. The referee then throws the basketball directly up between the two players who then try to bat it to the other members of their team. When a jump ball occurs, the other members of both teams must be outside of the center circle and may not interfere with the two jumpers. A jump ball is also repeated if the ball is batted out of bounds prior to it being touched by any other player, and it can't be determined which team had control of the ball.

Regulation Play

A ball is considered live when there is a jump ball, a free throw, or a throw-in. It can be dribbled, passed, thrown, bounced, tapped, rolled, or batted. It cannot be carried (it can be held) or kicked. A *player* is said to have control if he is holding or dribbling the ball. A *team* is said to have control of the ball when it is being passed between members. Control is lost when a basket is scored, the ball is dead, or it is stolen by the other team. A ball is considered dead when: a basket is made, there is a foul or violation, when a free throw is attempted, the ball goes out of bounds, the 30-second buzzer sounds, and finally if the clock runs out. If the game is over, the buzzer sounds, but if the ball is in flight during the buzzer, then it is not considered dead until it touches the basket, backboard, the floor, or a member of either team. Points are counted if the ball goes into the basket after the buzzer sounds.

Scoring

Two points are scored when a player shoots the ball from within the three-point line and the ball passes through the basket. If a basket is made from a shot that is outside of the three-point line then it is worth three points. Imagine that! A basket scored by a free throw is worth one point.

Restarting the Game After a Basket Has Been Scored

The scoring team cannot handle the ball after a basket has been scored. The referee must hand the ball to a member of the opposite team that will be throwing in the ball. When a player has possession of the ball, a throw-in must be performed within 5 seconds. After a basket has been scored the game officially resumes play when a member of the opposite team throws in the ball from behind the *end line.*

Throw-In

A throw-in is when a player from the team that was awarded the ball stands on the sideline where the ball went out of bounds. (The ball is thrown in from the end line after a basket has been scored.) The basketball is handed to the player by the referee and throw-ins must be completed within 5 seconds of this exchange. He may then throw or bounce the ball onto the court to a member of his team. The basketball must touch another player before the player who is throwing in the ball is allowed to touch it again.

Dribble

A basketball player moves the ball down the court by running and bouncing the ball between his hand and the floor. This bouncing motion is called a "dribble," and it must be done when the player is in motion.

Moving With the Ball

There are basically two times when a basketball player does not have to dribble the ball. The first is when a player is standing still, has possession of the ball, and is pivoting on one foot in order to attempt to get in a better position to either pass or shoot the ball. The second is when the player is attempting to shoot or pass the ball. This time frame starts with a two count rhythm that begins when the player takes possession of the ball and either leaps into the air or passes the ball. The first count is when the player takes control of the ball and his feet are touching the ground and the second count is when the player's feet touch the ground again. Example: For those of you who do not understand, (it's OK, it took me a while to figure this out) when a player has been passed the ball and he starts to run with it, he has to the count of two to start dribbling. He can also take two steps, while holding the ball when he is going up for a basket. Understand now?

Legal Guarding Position

A legal guarding position is taken when a defensive player is facing an offensive player, and has both feet on the floor.

Time-Outs

The official game clock stops when the referee indicates that there has been some type of violation, if he needs to suspend play due to an injury, or if he wishes to confer with other officials. Each team is allowed to call two time-outs of one minute each in each half. Time-outs that are not used in the first half cannot be carried over to the second half, and there is one time-out allowed per team if there is an overtime. The coach usually gives the signal for a time-out to the player who has possession of the ball, who in turn, calls the time-out with the referee. When a time-out is over, the game is resumed by either a throw-in by the team who had control of the ball prior to the time-out being called, or by a jump ball if neither team had control. (In the NBA a team gets six time-outs per game with a maximum of three in the fourth quarter and two in the final 2 minutes.)

Time Limitations

Thirty-Second Rule

When a team gains control of the ball, it has 30 seconds (24 seconds in the NBA) to try to shoot for a basket. A new 30-second period starts over if the ball goes out of bounds or a basket is made. The 30-second time period does continue if the ball comes in contact with an opponent, but the team keeps control of the ball.

Ten-Second Rule

When a team has possession of the ball in the backcourt (the backcourt is the half of the court that is farthest away from the basket they shoot at) the players have 10 seconds to move it into the frontcourt. It is illegal for the team that has possession of the ball to move the ball back into the backcourt once it has been moved into the frontcourt.

Three-Second Rule

No player can remain more than 3 seconds in the 4-foot restricted area between their opponent's end line and the free throw line, when his team has possession of the ball. However, this rule does not apply if the ball is in the air after being shot or rebounded. (I think it's a dumb rule.)

Rule Violations, Fouls, and Free Throws

When a team violates a rule, the ball is awarded to the other team. A foul is a violation that involves illegal contact between two players or unsportsmanlike behavior. If a shooting player is fouled but has also scored a basket, then that player attempts one free throw. If the player is fouled and the basket was *not* made, then two free throws are attempted. If there is a foul on players from both teams, then there is a jump ball.

A Free Throw

A free throw is taken after a technical or personal foul on a player who was in the act of shooting. If a personal foul was committed, then the fouled player takes the free throw shot. If the foul was a technical foul then any player on the opposing team may attempt the shot. The thrower stands right behind the free throw line, and the ball must be shot within 10 seconds once it has been passed to the player who is making the shot. The other players line up along the outside free throw lines with two members of the opposite team in the closest position to the basket. The other players alternate positions and cannot interfere with the player who is making the shot. They also must not attempt to take control of the ball until it has hit the backboard or the basket.

Free Throw Violations

If a player on the free thrower's team interferes with the ball during the free throw then a throw-in is awarded to the other team. If the opposite team interferes with the ball during the free throw then the throwing team is awarded another free throw. If both teams interfere with the ball then a jump ball takes place on the free throw line.

Interference

Players are not allowed to touch the basket or the backboard when the ball is in or touching the basket. A player is also not allowed to touch a ball that is in its downward flight before it touches the metal ring. Violations of this rule known as *goaltending* result in free throws.

Out of Bounds

When the basketball crosses any of the boundary lines then the ball is considered dead, and it is then awarded to the team that *did not* touch the ball last. The ball is then put back into play with a throw-in.

Held Ball

When two players are holding and fighting for the ball, officials will call a held ball. The ball is then considered dead and play resumes with a jump ball at the nearest circle.

Personal Fouls

A personal foul involves contact between two players whether the ball is in play or not. Players will be called for a personal foul for blocking, holding, pushing, charging, tripping, or using any uncalled for rough play. Contact with a player that is in the act of shooting the ball is illegal as well as contact with a player who is dribbling the ball and running up the court. An *intentional foul* is when a personal foul was obviously deliberately committed by a player, and a *disqualifying foul* is when the player is guilty of flagrant unsportsmanlike conduct. It is up to the referee to distinguish between the two and make the decision to remove a player from a game.

Technical Foul

Technical fouls can be committed by either the coach or a player. A technical foul is called on a player if he commits any of the following acts: uses abusive language, acts unsportsmanlike, delays the game, or taunts another player. In many cases the player is warned before being given a technical foul, and is only penalized if the foul is repeated. The team is penalized with a technical foul if the coach basically commits any of the same violations as his players. However, a foul can also be called if the coach crosses the boundaries and comes onto the court.

Double Foul

When two players on opposite teams foul at the same time then a double foul is called and the game is restarted with a jump ball.

Multiple Fouls

If two or more players foul against another player then a personal foul is recorded against each player and the player who was fouled on can take two free throws. If the player was fouled and scores a basket, then the basket counts and he is awarded one free throw.

Five Fouls

If a *player* has committed five fouls, either personal or technical, then that player is removed from the game and is replaced with a substitute.

Seven Fouls

If a *team* commits seven fouls, either personal or technical, in a single half then any additional fouls committed by the team are penalized by awarding the other team an additional free throw if the first free throw is good. (The one and one rule.) In the NBA it is anything in excess of four fouls per period.

51

Football

What is Football?

Football is blocking or tackling an opponent (depending on whether you are on offense or defense) in order to score points or to prevent the opponent from scoring. It is played by two teams each consisting of 11 players. The winner of the game is the team that has scored the most points within the allotted playing time. There is 60 minutes of actual playing time in professional football, and points are scored when the ball is legally moved on, over, or across the other team's goal line. The goal line is in the end zone.

The Playing Field

The playing field is 100 yards long and 53⅓ yards wide. The playing area is between the sidelines and the end lines, which are 10 yards behind the goal line. The end zone begins at the goal line and extends 10 yards to the end line. The field is divided between the goal lines in 1 yard intervals, and it is illegal to have anything fixed to the ground that is with in 5 yards of the sidelines.

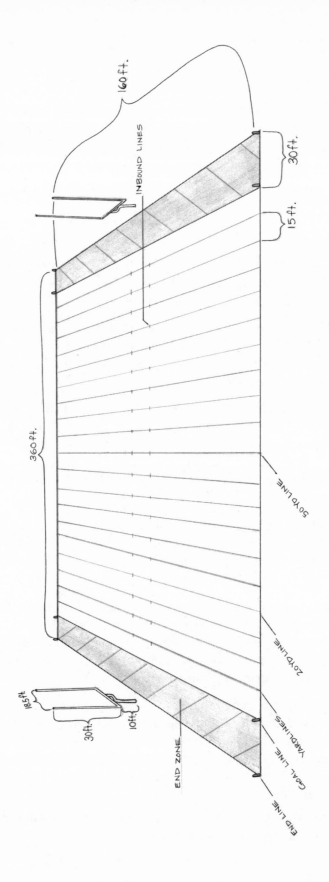

160 ft.

INBOUND LINES

30 ft.

15 ft.

360 ft.

50 yd LINE

END ZONE

20 yd LINE

18.5 ft.

30 ft.

10 ft.

YARD LINES

GOAL LINE

END LINE

The Officials

In professional football there are 7 officials who have different functions and responsibilities on the football field. All officials wear white pants and a black baseball hat except the referee who wears a white hat. Their shirts are white and black vertical stripes and each carries a whistle and a yellow flag.

The Referee is the chief official and is in charge of the game.

The Umpire is responsible for the teams equipment and the line of scrimmage.

The Head Linesman is in charge of offsides, the neutral zone, the chain crew, and keeping track of how far the ball has moved. He changes sides of the field at half time.

The Line Judge keeps track of forward passes, kicks, and loose balls. The line judge is on the opposite side of the field as the linesman and also keeps track of time, movements on the line of scrimmage, and any illegal team coverage.

The Field Judge works on the same side of the field as the line judge, 20 yards downfield (past the line of scrimmage). He keeps track of offensive and defensive players in his area and rules on whether catches are legal, possession or recovery of the ball, or if there is any interference or other infractions. With the back judge he also rules on the success of field goals.

The Side Judge works on the same side of the field as the linesman, 20 yards downfield. He has essentially the same duties as the field judge except he doesn't rule on field goals.

The Back Judge operates 25 yards downfield generally on the strong side (i.e., tight end's side of the field). He observes the tight end's actions and defensive players in his area and rules on whether catches are legal, possession or recovery of the ball, or if there is any interference or other infractions. He also keeps time on the intervals between downs and during halftime intermission.

In collegiate games there can be as few as four officials or as many as seven. All crews contain at least a referee, an umpire, a linesman, and a line judge, Other officials are added according to the budget and rules of the various conferences.

Teams and Players

There are two teams of eleven players. Each team may not have more than 45 players in uniform and ready to play on the sidelines at any time.

Unlimited substitution is allowed but may only be done when the ball is out of play.

Offense

The offensive is the team that has control of the ball and is trying to move it down the field and to the other team's goal line and into the end zone. The offensive positions and basic job duties are:

Quarterback The quarterback is the player that starts the game in play and then either passes or hands off the ball to the backs or ends or may run with it himself.

Center The center hikes the ball to the quarterback when the quarterback has given the signal to start the play of the game and then blocks opposing players.

Guard There are two guards on the left and right of the center. The job of these guys is to block the defense and protect the quarterback.

Tackle Next to the guards there are two tackles who basically have the same job as the guards.

End Next to the tackles are the ends. Ends can be either tight ends or wide receivers. The ends have a duel job and can either run down the field so the quarterback can throw the ball to them, or can act as blockers to assist the guards and tackles.

Backs Finally, there are three backs (halfback, fullback, and tailback) that can either run with or catch the ball and block for the quarterback. These players along with the ends can be put "in motion" (i.e., move out of a set position) before the ball is snapped, however they are not allowed to cross the line of scrimmage until the ball has been snapped.

The basic offense can be varied by putting in four wide receivers and taking out two backs; by putting in two tight ends, two wide receivers, and one back; or by putting a back on the line of scrimmage to act as a wide receiver.

Defense

The defense is the team that tries to prevent the offense from crossing their goal line. The defensive players are:

Defensive Tackle There are two defensive tackles who usually line up opposite to and between the center and the guards. They try to cross the line of scrimmage and stop the offense's play.

Defensive End The defensive ends line up opposite to and between the guards and the tackles. Sometimes they will line up outside the offensive tackles. They have the same job as the defensive tackles.

Linebacker There are usually three linebackers and can line up in any number of positions on the field. They usually take a position near wherever they think the ball will be played. Their primary concern is to stop the player who has the ball or to defend passes.

Defensive Back There are four defensive backs (two cornerbacks and two safeties) who chuck (ward off by a quick extension of the arm) and cover the ends and the running backs. Their primary concern is to protect against passes from the quarterback to these players farther down the field. They also help on run defense when in a position to do so.

The basic defense can be varied by putting in three defensive linemen (two defensive ends and a nose tackle), four linebackers, and four defensive backs; four defensive linemen, two linebackers, and five defensive backs (called a nickel package); or three defensive linemen, two linebackers, and six defensive backs (called a dime package).

Uniforms

The only major restriction (other than not having razor blades embedded in a players arm pads) is that a team's jersey cannot be a color similar to the actual football. The numbers on the jerseys measure 8 inches high on the chest, and 10 inches high on the back. Traditionally centers are numbered 50–79, guards and tackles 60–79, ends 80–89 (alternatively 10–19), defensive backs and running backs 10–49, linebackers 50–59 (alternatively 90–99), defensive linemen 90–99 (alternatively 60–79), and quarterbacks, punters, and kickers 1–19. Each player must wear: a helmet with a face mask, chest and shoulder pads, rib and kidney pads, pants with thigh and shin pads, a cup, and cleats.

The Ball

The football is an oblong inflated rubber bladder that is encased in leather. It is 11–11¼ inches long, has a circumference between 28–28½ inches at its widest part, and weighs about 14–15 ounces.

Length of Play, Time Outs, and Overtime

There are 60 minutes of actual playing time that is divided into four quarters, and two halves. Playing time excludes any time-outs and when the ball is considered dead or out of play. There is a 2 minute break between each quarter, and a 12 minute break at the half. Each team has three time-outs during each half that last 40 seconds unless the time-out is for a TV commercial, then it is 1 minute 50 seconds. Time-outs are made at the team captain's request. A time-out does not apply if a player is injured, however, that player must leave the field for at least one play. If the original 60 minutes runs out and the game is tied, then there is a 15-minute overtime period. The kickoff is determined by another coin toss, and the game is won by the first team to score any points (known as *sudden death*). If neither side scores in the 15-minute time period the game ends in a tie.

Playing the Game

The official rules state that 3 minutes before the game the team captains flip a coin to determine who receives the kickoff. The visiting team captain calls the toss, and the winner of the coin toss has the choice of either kicking off to the other team or receiving the kickoff. The loser of the coin toss is given the opportunity to choose which goal his team wants to defend. The captain who lost the coin toss at the start of the game is given the choice of kicking off or receiving the kickoff at the start of the second half. The teams switch ends of the field at the end of the first and third quarter, but the position of the ball, and the down remains the same.

Kickoffs

The game is started with a kickoff on the 30-yard line at the start of each half, after a field goal, or after an extra point; or with a *safety kick* on the 20-yard line after a safety (a.k.a. a *free kick*). The football can be kicked off in the following ways: The ball can be drop-kicked (dropped on the ground and kicked on the rebound), another player may hold the ball on the ground for a place kick, or it can be kicked off a 1-inch tee. A safety kick is a punt kick, however it is only allowed from the 20-yard line after a safety. The kicking team, except for the actual kicker and the person holding the ball, must be behind the ball. The opposing team must be at least 10 yards away from the kicking team. When the ball is kicked off it must travel at least 10 yards, then it is considered in play and can be run downfield. If the kicking team gains control of the ball (an *onside kick*) then the ball is dead, but the kicking team has control of the ball at the point of where it was recovered. If the ball is kicked out of bounds during a kickoff and the ball was never touched, then the kicking team is penalized. The receiving team can either take the ball at the yard line where it went out of bounds, or they can take it on their 35-yard line, whichever is farther downfield. Nine times out of ten it will be taken at the 35-yard line. Did you catch all that?

Fair Catch

During a kickoff or a punt any of the receiving team's players may claim the right to catch the ball by raising one hand above his head. That player can then catch the ball without the fear of being tackled or blocked. When he catches the ball it becomes dead on that spot. Once a player has signaled a fair catch, it is illegal for him to attempt to run down the field.

Ball Movement

When a team has possession of the ball it has four downs (tries) in which to advance 10 yards ahead. If the team advances that distance it is given another four downs. If the ball is not moved 10 yards in four downs then the ball is awarded to the opposing team from the point at which it became dead. The ball can be legally moved by running, passing, or kicking. Generally, if a team has not made 10 yards in three downs, on fourth down they will punt the ball away to the opposition to move the ball down the field away from their goal (see Kicking).

Passing

Forward Pass When the ball is in play the team who has possession of the ball is allowed one forward pass. The player who is performing the pass must be behind the line of scrimmage at the time of the pass, and any other forward pass by either team is illegal. All defensive players are eligible to catch a forward pass, but the only offensive players that are eligible to catch the ball are located at the end of the line of scrimmage (these players are called the *ends*) or behind the scrimmage line. If a player of the opposing team touches the ball then all players of the passing team are allowed to touch the ball and advance it. If the opposing team catches the ball it is called an *interception* and is now in possession of that team. A forward pass is dead if it is thrown out of bounds, hits the ground, or hits the goal post.

Backward Pass Any player in legal possession of the ball may pass the ball backward to another player at anytime.

Kicking

There are basically four types of kicks in American football. The *kickoff* (See Kickoff), the *field goal* (see Scoring), the *extra point* (see Scoring), and the *punt*. The punt is usually performed on the fourth down when the team who has possession of the ball has no chance of advancing the ball the required minimum of 10 yards. Unlike other kicks, the ball does not touch the ground but is dropped in the air over the punter's foot and kicked away.

Running

The player who has possession of the ball may run anywhere on the playing field that he wishes, just as long as he stays inbounds, until he is tackled or scores.

When Is the Ball Considered Dead or Out of Play?

The ball is dead when one of the officials blows his whistle. This can happen after a foul, after a team scores, after an incomplete pass, after a player with the ball is tackled to the ground, or after the ball goes out of bounds. It can be kicked out of bounds, passed out of bounds, or run out of bounds. The next play is then restarted at the point where the ball was last inbounds.

Scoring

Touchdown (Six points) A touchdown occurs when the football is on, over, or across the goal line of the opposing team's end zone. The ball can be carried into the end zone, caught in the end zone, or a player may recover a loose ball on or behind the opponent's goal line.

Extra point (One or two points) After a touchdown is scored the scoring team is given the opportunity to score either one or two additional points. A scrimmage takes place between the goal line and the 2-yard line. One point is scored if the scoring team kicks the ball through the goal posts, or two points are scored if the ball is run into or caught in the end zone. The play is over as soon as the opposing team touches the ball or tackles the opposing team member who has control of the ball.

Field Goal (Three points) A field goal occurs when a player placekicks or drop-kicks the ball through the opposing team's goal posts from behind the line of scrimmage. He may not punt the ball or throw it through the goal posts.

Safety (Two points) A safety occurs when a team possesses the ball in its own end zone and the ball is downed behind the goal line. For example, the quarterback is sacked in his own end zone or the ball is fumbled out of bounds behind the goal line. It is also awarded to the other team if the team in possession of the ball commits a foul behind its own goal line.

Fouls

Even though football is a very violent game there are rules. No player is allowed to hit, kick, or knee another player, and stiffer penalties are usually imposed if an opponent is hit in the head or neck. Kicking is defined as when a player is hit above the knee by the foot of another player and tripping a running player is also illegal. Players can't tackle another player who is out of bounds, pile on top of a player when the ball is out of play, or continue to try to tackle a player after the ball is dead. Defensive players may not use the palms of their hands above the offensive players shoulders, except to ward him off during the initial charge at the line of scrimmage. A defensive player may not intentionally tackle or run into a kicker or try to tackle the passer after the ball has left his hands. It is illegal for any player, from either team to cross the line of scrimmage prior to the ball being snapped, or to grab any player by the face mask. Finally, it is illegal for football players to, believe it or not, behave in an unsportsmanlike manner.

Penalties

When a player commits a foul there are two basic punishments that can be imposed: either the loss of a down or loss of either 5, 10, or 15 yards or both loss of down and penalty yards. These penalties can be given either one at a time or in combination. It is also possible, if the offense is severe enough, that the player, the coach, or the team is disqualified.

Definitions

Blocking Blocking is the use of the body above the knees by a player who is trying to obstruct an opponent. Players can block an opponent at any time as long as it doesn't interfere with a fair pass or a fair kick. It is illegal to block below the knees or block into a player's back.

Dead Ball When the player who has possession of the ball touches the ground with any part of his body, except his hands or feet, an incomplete pass, the ball goes out of bounds, the team scores, or a foul occurs, then the ball is considered dead, and another play begins.

Defensive Player A defensive player tries to prevent the opponents from scoring. The only person a defensive player can tackle or hold is the person who has control of the ball. He can use his hands, arms, and body to evade or get around the blocking opponent.

Fumble When a player has possession and then loses possession of the ball when it is in play, it is considered a fumble. Whoever gains control of the ball first has possession.

Line of Scrimmage Each team lines up at least seven players on either side of the ball. The lines where each team gets into place is called the line of scrimmage. The area between the two teams is called the neutral zone and is the length of the football.

Offensive Player An offensive player tries to score points or can assist the person who has control of the ball by blocking defensive players.

He may use his hands and arms to block, but he can't push, lift, grasp, or tackle the opponent. When a receiver is within 5 yards of the line of scrimmage, he can be chucked by any defender prior to having control of the ball.

Scrimmage When the ball is snapped and play begins this is called a scrimmage.

Snap The snap is the backward pass through the legs of the center. This movement puts the ball in play. The snap must be one continuous action, and all players who are lined up on their respective lines of scrimmage may not move until this ball movement is made. The snap must be made to a player who is behind the line of scrimmage, usually the quarterback.

Tackling The use of their hands, arms, and body by a defensive player to stop the offensive player from advancing any farther down the field.

52

Soccer

What Is Soccer?

Soccer is kicking, heading, or propelling the ball with any part of your body except your hands and arms (except for the goalkeeper). It is a game played by two teams consisting of eleven players. The object of the game is to put the ball into the opponent's goal, and the winning team is the one that has scored the greatest number of goals.

The Ball

The ball is spherical, 27–28 inches in circumference, weighs 14–16 ounces, and is covered in leather.

The Field

A soccer field is rectangular and can actually vary in size. However, it must measure between 50–100 yards wide and 100–130 yards long. On average, the size of a professional soccer field is 80 yards wide and 110 yards long.

The **goal** is 8 feet high and 8 yards wide and is in the center of the field on the goal line (the end line across the width of the field). The frame is made of wood or metal and cannot be more than 5 inches wide or thick. Attached to the frame is a net. The **goal area** is marked by white lines 6 yards out toward the touch lines (the boundary lines that mark the length

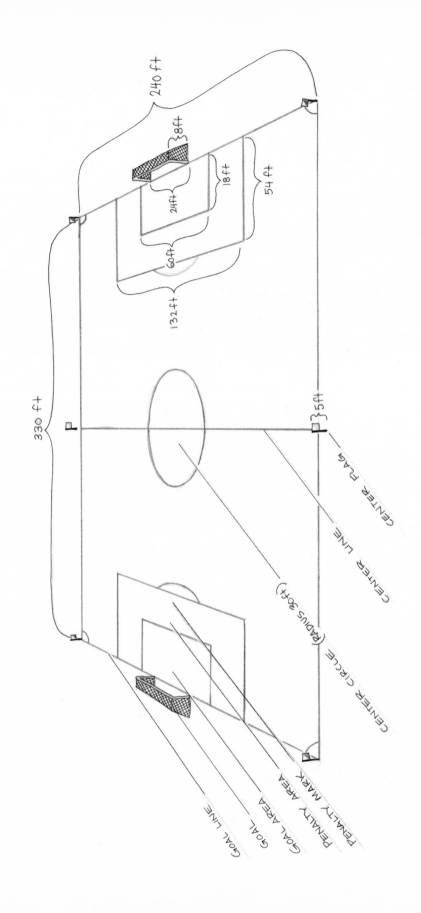

240 ft

}8ft

18 ft

54 ft

24ft

60ft

132 ft

330 ft

}5 ft

CENTER FLAG

CENTER LINE

CENTER CIRCLE (RADIUS 30ft)

GOAL LINE

GOAL AREA

PENALTY AREA

PENALTY MARK

of the field) and 6 yards out from the goal onto the field forming a box around the goal. The **penalty area** is another box marked with a white line 18 yards out from the goal line toward the touch lines and 18 yards out from the goal onto the field.

Officials

There are three officials who make rule decisions during a soccer game. There is a **referee** who is in control of the game and makes calls from the actual playing field. He also keeps track of the playing time, enforces the rules, and stops the game when there are infringements or injuries. There are also two **assistant referees or linesmen** who are stationed on both sides of the field. The job of the linesmen is to determine when the ball is out of play and to rule as to which team has the right to put the ball back into play with either a throw-in, corner kick, or goal kick. The linesmen can also make calls on any rule violations that they see, but it is up to the referee to make the final decision on their calls.

Players

There are ten players on a soccer team and one goalkeeper. At the beginning of the game three players, called **forwards**, line up right behind the center line. The **forwards** or **strikers** are usually the fastest players and run with the ball to try to score goals. Three players, called **midfielders or half backs,** line up about 15–20 yards behind the forwards. They have similar offensive duties as the forwards and also score goals. Next, there are four **full backs or defenders** that line up in front of the penalty area and the goalkeeper. Their primary function is defending the goal and preventing the ball from getting to the goalkeeper. Finally, the last line of defense is the **goalkeeper**. His only job is to defend the goal. This player can use his hands, but not beyond the penalty area around his goal.

Substitutes

There is a maximum of two substitutes that are permitted in a soccer game. Substitutes have to be named before the game, and once a player has been substituted that player is not allowed to return to the game. The referee has to be notified prior to the substitutes taking the field. If a player has been ordered off the field by the referee due to a violation after the game has started, that player cannot be replaced.

Length of Play

A game is played in two halves of 45 minutes each. The teams change sides at the end of the halves and the time between these halves cannot be longer than 15 minutes except if the referee makes the decision to alter it. Since the referee keeps time only he can add any additional time to a half, usually for time lost from injuries, wasted time, or penalty kicks. This is called **stoppage time** and its length is announced at the end of the half.

Control of the Ball

Except when a player has to pick up the ball to perform a throw-in, the goalkeeper is the only player allowed to use his hands and arms during regular play. A player can use his feet, legs, head, and chest to control the ball and move it downfield.

Scoring and Winning

A goal is scored when the soccer ball has completely crossed the goal line, and goes into the goal. The team that scores the greatest number of goals before time runs out, wins. If at the end of the game there is a tie score then, depending on the type of game being played, it is ended in a draw or there is overtime. In professional games there is usually overtime that consists of two 15-minute halves. In championship games these may be "sudden death" or "golden goal" (i.e., the team that scores first wins) overtimes. In championship play, if after two overtimes the score is still tied then the teams go to a "shoot out"; each team gets five penalty shots to determine a winner. Minor or little league games are usually ended in a tie.

Uniform

All players must wear a jersey that has a number on the back, shorts, shinguards, socks, and cleats. Cleats are basically running shoes with rubber studs on the bottom. The studs cannot be more than ¾ of an inch in length and not less than ½ inch in diameter. The goalkeeper must wear a jersey that is a different color so he can be distinguished from the rest of his team, and he can also wear gloves for better grip when handling the ball. No player is allowed to wear anything that could possibly be used to injure another player, and any player found to be wearing dangerous equipment can be ejected from the game.

Starting the Game

Prior to the game the two team captains flip a coin to determine which team will defend which goal, and also which team will kick off. After the coin toss the team that is kicking off puts the ball in play from a stationary kick from the center of the center line. The kickoff must be a forward kick that crosses over into the opponent's half of the field, and the player making the initial kick may not touch the ball again until it has been touched by another player. No player from the other team is allowed to enter the center circle until the ball is put into play. The game is physically started and the kickoff is taken after the referee blows his whistle.

Out of Play

The ball is considered out of play when either the referee has stopped the game, or the ball crosses the touch lines or the goal lines. The game is then restarted when either the referee drops the ball back into play (see restarting games) or a member of one of the teams performs a throw-in, a corner kick, or a goal kick.

Offsides

An offensive player is considered offsides when the ball is put into play by his team and that player is nearer to the other team's goal than the ball and *two* members of the other team. He would not be considered offsides if: he is in his half of the field, a member of the other team was the last person to touch the ball, or he receives the ball as a result of a corner kick, goal kick, or throw-in. Although a player may be technically considered offsides the referee may not make the call if the player is not directly interfering with the play of the game or is not at an advantage by being in that position.

Restarting Games

After a goal has been scored the game is restarted the same way, but the team that was scored upon will be making the kick. The second half is started by a kickoff by the team that did not start the first half. If the referee stops the game and there is no reason to award a free kick to either team, (for example, if there is an injury) then the referee may restart the game by dropping the ball at the place where it was when the play was stopped. Players from either team may not attempt to take control of the ball until it has touched the ground.

Throw-In

A throw-in is taken at the side line at the point where the ball went out of bounds. The throw-in is performed by a member of the team that *did not* touch the ball last. For example if a member of team "A" touched the ball last before it went out of bounds, then a member of team "B" will perform the throw-in. The ball must be thrown back into play with both hands, from behind and over the head. The thrower must face the field and both feet must be on the ground either on or behind the sidelines. If any of those guidelines are not met then the throw-in is no good and it is awarded to the opposing team. A goal cannot be scored directly from a throw-in (i.e., it can't be thrown into the goal) and the player who performed the throw-in cannot touch the ball again until it has been touched by another player.

Goal Kick

A goal kick is given to the defending team when the ball crosses their goal line and the last person to touch the ball is a member of the offensive team. This type of kick can be taken by any member of the team, usually the goal-keeper. The ball is kicked from the half of the goal area nearest to where the ball crossed the goal line. All players must be out of the penalty area prior to a goal kick being taken. Also, the player performing the goal kick must kick it hard enough so that it is sent out of the penalty area, and the kicker cannot touch the ball again until it has been touched by another player. A goal *can* be scored directly from a goal kick into the opponent's goal.

Corner Kick

A corner kick is given to the offensive team when the ball crosses the goal line and the last person to touch the ball was a member of the defending team. A corner kick is taken from the corner of the field on the side where the ball crossed the goal line. All players must stand at least 10 yards away from the person performing the corner kick, and the person performing the corner kick cannot touch the ball again until it has been touched by another player. A goal *can* be scored directly from a corner kick.

Fouls and Free Kicks

Direct Free or Penalty Kick

A direct free kick is awarded to the opposing team if any of ten fouls (listed below) are committed against a player. The ball is placed at the spot of the foul and all opposing players must move back 10 yards from the ball. The ball *can* be kicked directly into the goal and score. A penalty kick is awarded if any of the ten fouls are committed in the penalty area.

A penalty kick is taken from the penalty mark (12 yards out from the middle of the goal), and a goal *can* be scored from a penalty kick. All play-ers, except the goalkeeper must stand outside of the penalty area at least 10 yards from the penalty mark. The player taking the kick must kick the ball forward only, and he cannot touch the ball again until it has been touched by another player. The goalkeeper must remain on his goal line, facing the kicker, between the goal posts until the ball has been put in motion. The goalkeeper may move laterally but *not* forward.

Fouls That Result in Direct Free or Penalty Kicks

A direct free kick is awarded to the other team if one of the following intentional fouls was committed by a player:

1. Tripping an opponent.
2. Holding an opponent.
3. Using the hands or arms (except the goalkeeper).
4. Kicking an opponent.
5. Jumping on an opponent.
6. Charging violently at an opponent.
7. Pushing an opponent.
8. Spitting on an opponent.
9. Striking an opponent or attempting to do so.
10. Tackling an opponent and making contact with the opponent. before touching the ball.

Indirect Free Kick

An indirect free kick is one from which a goal *cannot* be scored until the ball has been touched by another player. All opponents must be at least 10 yards from the ball, and if the defending side is given a free kick in its own penalty area then the ball must be kicked out of the penalty area and no opponents may enter that area.

Fouls That Result in an Indirect Free Kick

An indirect free kick is awarded to the other team if one of the following intentional fouls was committed by a player:

1. Dangerous play.
2. Obstructing the opponent.
3. When a player is offsides.
4. When the goalkeeper wastes time or plays around with the ball more than 6 seconds.
5. When the goalkeeper releases the ball from his hands and retouches it with his hands before another player touches the ball, or touches the ball with his hands after it has been kicked to him by a teammate or directly from a throw-in by a teammate.
6. When a player after performing a throw-in, goal kick, or a corner kick touches the ball prior to the ball touching another player.
7. When the game has been stopped to reprimand a player.

Free kicks are retaken if:

1. The defending team breaks a rule and a goal is *not* scored.
2. The attacking team breaks a rule and a goal *is* scored.
3. There are rules broken by both teams.
4. If the kicker breaks a rule, then an indirect free kick is awarded to the other team.

Cautioning and Ejecting Players

A referee can caution or eject a player if he:

1. Continuously breaks the rules.
2. Is guilty of unsportsmanlike conduct.
3. Uses foul language.
4. Enters or leaves a game without the referee's permission.
5. Verbally or physically opposes any of the decisions made by the referee.
6. Commits any acts of violence.

When a player is cautioned for the first time he is given a **yellow card.** If he is cautioned again, he is given a second yellow card and then immediately a **red card,** and the player is ejected. If a referee thinks a violation is severe enough, then the yellow card may be passed over and the player can be given a red card on his first violation.

53

Golf

Golf is simply hitting a ball with a club into a series of holes, and the person who has to hit that ball the least number of times wins. It can be played alone, but also played in groups of two, three, or four. There are two forms of the game.

Match Play—Match play means that the team winning the majority of holes wins the game. A match usually consists of a certain number of holes. It can be that each hole is a match or there can be three-hole matches, even four-hole matches. Teams can consist of one or more people.

Stroke Play—Stroke play means that the winner of the game is the player who finishes with the lowest number of strokes (swings at the ball) for the whole course. This game can be played with teams as well.

The lowest score of one of the partners is used as the score for a particular hole. For example, if Joe and Bob are on a team and Joe hits a 4 on a par 5 hole, while Bob hits a 6, the team will use Joe's score for their team's score.

Clubs

There are basically three types of clubs a player can use: a wood, an iron, and a putter. The total number of clubs a player can use is fourteen. However, a player can replace damaged clubs during a game or add new clubs if he started with less than fourteen. Each club, with the exception of the putter, has only one striking face. The face of the club is allowed to be indented or scored, but it is not allowed to be finished in a way so that it will effect the distance the ball is hit. The length of the club's shaft and the angle of the club's head vary from club to club. The higher the number of the club the sharper the club's head angle. Steeply angled club heads give sharper lifting shots.

Wood A wood usually has the longest shaft. The head is broad from front to back and is made of wood, plastic, and metal. Woods are numbered from 1 to 9 and are used for long shots.

Iron An iron's shaft is a little shorter than that of a wood, and the head is relatively narrow. Irons are made of steel and are numbered from 1 to 10. Irons are to be used for medium and short shots. The 10 iron is also know as a **wedge,** and the club after the 10 iron is called the **sand wedge.** These clubs are designed so that when the ball is hit it will have a higher yet shorter trajectory. They are the clubs you use when you have to get your ball out of a sand trap or an obstacle that you have to hit the ball over.

Putter The putter is a light metal club used to hit the ball when it is on the green. Unlike woods and irons there is usually no angle to the putter's club head.

Course

A standard golf course is eighteen holes that vary in length from 100 to 600 yards. Each of the eighteen holes will contain the following attributes:

1. **Teeing Ground** A rectangular starting area on which the ball is hit from a tee.
2. **Fairway** A closely mowed length of grass that players use for aim when they hit the ball.
3. **Rough** Unkept areas on the sides of the fairway containing high grass, brush, or trees.

4. **Hazards** Areas of the fairway that the golfer wants to avoid. The most common are sand bunkers and water hazards.
5. **Putting Green** A smooth area on which the hole is located.

Each course will have its own conditions, but they all must have clearly defined boundaries.

Scoring

The player who completes each hole or all 18 holes with the least number of strokes is the winner.

> **Par** Par is calculated based on the length and difficulty of a hole. Par is usually calculated from 3–5 and is the number of strokes that a perfect player would need to complete the hole.
>
> **Birdie** One stroke under par.
>
> **Eagle** Two strokes under par.
>
> **Bogie** One stroke over par.

Handicap

Handicaps are based on the par for a course. A man can receive a handicap of up to 24 while a woman can receive a handicap of up to 36. Basically, a handicap is how much a player usually hits over par for the course. For example, if par for an 18-hole course is 72 and the player hits an 80 then his handicap is 8.

Playing the Ball

Each player starts a hole from the teeing ground. The ball is either placed on a small pile of sand, or on a wooden or plastic tee.

> **Off Tee**—If the ball falls off the tee before a stroke, there is no penalty, if the ball falls off the tee during a stroke there is no penalty, however, that stroke does count.

There is no specific order of who goes first other than what your teams decide on. Once the ball has been hit from the teeing area, the ball must be played from the point of where it landed from that shot, and it must be played as it lies. The ball cannot be moved or touched, and a player can't try to improve his shot by moving, bending, or breaking anything that is in the way of his shot. The player also cannot move or step on any dirt or loose turf. The player can make these adjustment if it is in reference to his stance or swing. For example, he can bend a branch to swing his club. A player can also move anything that has fallen into his path. For example, a tree branch that has fallen onto the green.

Practice—players are allowed practice swings but are not allowed practice strokes. For example, you can't hit the ball and say that it was just a practice shot.

Order—Other than teeing off, where it is up to the team to choose who goes first, in general rules of play the ball farthest from the hole is played first. If a player goes out of turn and you are playing match play, then the other team may require you to replay the stroke; in stroke play the game continues with no penalty.

The Stroke

The ball must be hit with the head of the club, it can't be pushed, scooped, or spooned. A player can't hit a ball twice. If he does, the stroke counts, and a penalty stroke is added. A player cannot move a ball unless it is in water or it moves after the stroke begins.

The Putt

The intended path of the putt cannot be interfered with, but rocks, leaves, and branches that have come to rest on the green can be moved. If there is something in the line of the putt that cannot be moved, such as an animal hole or standing water, the ball can be moved so that it will avoid this obstruction, but it can't be moved any closer to the hole. The player can clean his ball at this time and he can also repair any damage to the green that the impact of the ball may have caused. When putting, a player or caddie cannot test the surface of the green by rolling another ball, and while a ball is in motion no other balls can be touched or moved on the green. If the ball is in motion and something interferes with its expected line of travel, (like if a tree falls on the ball), then the stroke is canceled and the ball is replayed from the original spot. There is no penalty for this type of interference. If a ball hangs over the edge of the hole for more than ten seconds, then it is ruled to be at rest. If at a later time the ball falls into the hole, the player is said to have "holed" and another stroke is added to his score.

Obstructions and Hazards

Water Hazards The only time a ball can be moved is if it has landed in a water hazard. A player may search in the water for his ball, and will be given no penalty if he moves it. If the ball is lost, then the player may drop a ball with a one stroke penalty. The ball must be dropped as near as possible to the point from which the ball was played.

Bunkers Bunkers are areas of bare ground covered with a deep layer of sand. Balls cannot be moved from bunkers.

Rough "In the rough" usually means that the ball has been hit into the woods or into long grass and bushes.

Interference Interference occurs when something happens to the ball while it is in play that causes it to not continue in the same trajectory. For example, the ball hits a tree, a person, or a bird. The ball must be played from where it lies.

Definitions, Terms, and Rules

The Ball The ball has a maximum weight of 1.62 ounces, and it is 1.68 inches in diameter. The dimples in the ball makes the ball behave as if it were spherically symmetrical, and also improve accuracy and distance.

Ball at Rest When a ball is not moving and is not in play, it is called a ball at rest.

Caddie Each player is allowed one assistant called a caddie that can carry his golf bag and clubs, mark the position of the ball, and give the player advice.

Dropping the Ball Dropping the ball is done when the ball has to be repositioned (for example, if it is lost in a water hazard) and can only be done by the player himself. The player must stand up straight, hold the ball at shoulder height, and at arms length, and drop it. If any other method is used then the player is given a penalty stroke. A ball must be dropped as near as possible to the point where it went out of bounds, or was lost, but not any closer to the hole.

The Flag Stick The flag stick is placed in the center of the hole and is used to show the location of the hole when a player tees off. A flagstick may be removed when a player is preparing to putt, and a flag stick is said to be attended when it is being held by another player or caddie. If a ball strikes a flag stick or the flag stick attendant then the penalty is: for match play—loss of the hole, and stroke play—two strokes.

The Hole The standard measurement for a hole is 4¼ inches diameter, and 4 inches deep.

Lifting and Placing When a ball is on the green it may be lifted by the player himself or the players' caddie. The purpose of lifting is to move the other players' balls out of the way of the player that is getting ready to putt. Placing is when the ball is put back in its place when it is your turn to putt.

Lost or Unplayable Balls If a ball is lost or unplayable then it may be replaced with a "provisional" or replacement ball. The ball must be placed as near as possible where the ball went out of bounds, or was lost.

Provisional Ball A provisional ball is a replacement ball for a ball that is lost. A player has 5 minutes to search for his original ball. If the original ball is found right after the provisional ball is hit and it is not out of bounds, then the provisional ball is ignored, and the original ball is put back into play.

Moving Ball When a ball is in play, it is a moving ball.

54

Poker

Poker can be an exciting game, but that usually depends on if you are winning or not. If you just lost $1,000, it probably would not be considered much fun. There are two basic ingredients to playing poker. One I can teach you, the other I cannot. The part I can teach is which combinations of cards beats other combinations of cards (Hand Rankings) and the rules of the different games. The part I can't teach is knowing how long to stay in a game or bluffing. Kenny Rogers sang it best, "You have to know when to hold 'em and know when to fold 'em."

Hand Rankings

1. **Straight Flush** Five cards of the *same suit* in order. For example, 8, 7, 6, 5, 4 of Spades. A straight flush is ranked by the top card. If you have A, K, Q, J, 10 of a suit this is called a **Royal Flush.** The Ace can also be played as a low card; 5, 4, 3, 2, A is the lowest straight flush. In the event of a tie, the suit of the cards is not taken into consideration to break the tie. The pot is split equally between the winners.
2. **Four of a Kind** Four cards of the same rank. The fifth card doesn't really matter in this hand. It is called a high card or kicker, for example, 7, 7, 7, 7, 2.
3. **Full House** Three cards of one rank, followed by two of another, for example, 9, 9, 9, K, K. Full houses are ranked by the three cards, for example, a 9, 9, 9, K, K beats an 8, 8, 8, A, A.
4. **Flush** Five cards of the same suit, for example, J, 9, 7, 3, 2 of Diamonds. A flush is ranked by the top card so that an A,8,6,4,2 of a suit beats K, 8, 5, 4, 2.

5. **Straight** Five cards in numerical sequence, for example, 7, 6, 5, 4, 3.
6. **Three of a Kind** Three cards of the same rank and two extra cards, for example, Q, Q, Q, 8, 3.
7. **Two Pair** Two cards of one rank and two cards of another, and an extra card, for example, 10, 10, 6, 6, J. Two pair is ranked by the top pair and so on; for example, A, A, 4, 4, 2 beats Q, Q, 6, 6, 4.
8. **One Pair** Two cards of one rank and three extra cards, for example, 6, 6, K, J, 3.
9. **High Card** If you do not have any of the above combinations, the highest ranking card in your hand is used. Suits are not used to break ties.

Jokers and Wild Cards

When a Joker is in play it can only be used as an Ace or to complete a straight or flush. It is not considered a true wild card and can't be used in other ways. For example, if you have K, K, 2, 4, X (X= Joker), you can't try to play your hand as three Kings.

Wild Cards—Wild cards are rarely used in casinos, but they are often used in home games to add a little variety. A wild card is designated by the dealer, for example deuces wild, and any deuce can be used in place of any card. If a wild card is used then there is a new hand introduced into the game, five of a kind. Five of a kind ranks above the straight flush and becomes the highest ranking hand. If two players have five of a kind of the same rank, for example, if deuces and one-eyed jacks are wild and the hands come out K, K, 2, 2, 2 and 2, J, J, K, K then the players split the pot.

Betting

Poker players bet into a communal pot during the course of a hand, and the player holding the best hand at the end of the game wins the pot. Betting starts with the person to the left of the dealer and proceeds in a clockwise direction. There are different types of poker games that can have several betting rounds so there is not set number of times a player will have to bet. Usually the betting proceeds until each player has called all bets or has folded. During any betting round the players can do one of four things:

1. **Check** The bettor passes or declines to bet, but does not forfeit interest in the pot. For example, if the dealer goes to the first player and asks him what he wants to bet, he can check. However, if other players bet, he has to match that bet to stay in the pot.
2. **Bet** The initial wager put into the pot by the player that opens the betting.

3. **Call** A bet equal to a preceding bet that maintains a player's interest in the pot.
4. **Raise** A bet that increases the amount of the bet by at least as much as the previous bet. For example, if $5 is bet, then the raise must be $10 ($5 for the bet and $5 for the raise).
5. **Fold** To fold means a player is surrendering his interest in the pot, usually because his cards stink and he knows he can't win.

Rules of the Game

There numerous ways to play poker but these are the three most common versions that are played in casinos:

Five Card Draw This is the most common version and is played as follows: The dealer deals each player five cards one at a time starting from his left side and moving in a clockwise direction. After the cards are dealt there is a betting round, again starting with the person to the dealer's left. After the betting round the players are asked if they want to discard any cards. The maximum number of cards the players discard varies from three to all five, but this depends on house rules. There is no obligation to discard any. The discarded cards are traded for the same number of new cards. After the players have gotten their new cards there is another betting round. After the final betting round the players show their cards, and the winner collects the pot.

Seven Card Stud In seven card stud players are dealt two cards face down, then a third card face up. There is a betting round and all remaining players are dealt three more cards face up, with a betting round between each deal. After the fourth face-up card has been dealt, there is another betting round and then another card is dealt face down. Even though seven cards were dealt only five can be used to make a player's hand. This version of poker is called stud, because unlike five card draw you never draw cards.

Texas Hold 'Em Texas Hold 'Em is played by having each player dealt two cards face down. Then there is a betting round and then three community cards are dealt face up in the middle of the table. The community cards are cards that can be used in any player's hand. (The players use the two cards that were dealt to them, and the community cards to form the best hand possible.) After the three community cards are dealt there is another betting round, and then another community card is dealt. Again there is another betting round, then the last community card is dealt. Finally, another betting round. Using the five exposed cards in the middle of the table and the two in their possession, players form the best five-card hand that they believe will beat the other players.

55

Blackjack

Unlike poker, blackjack is a game where the players play against the dealer (also called the bank) and not against each other. The goal of the people playing blackjack is to draw cards that amount to 21 or as close to 21 as possible without going over. The following are the rules of the game according to Las Vegas Strip Rules:

Dealer Rules

The rules of the dealer are simple. The dealer has to draw until he has 17 or higher and also must stay when he reaches 17 or higher. These are specific guidelines and dealers must follow them. (Even if the dealer has 16 he has to draw.) The dealer does not have the freedom to draw cards depending on your hand or his gut feeling. If the dealer draws cards and goes over the sum of 21 he loses and all players, who still have a hand, win.

How the Game Is Played

Each player and the dealer are dealt two cards. One card is dealt face up and one card is dealt face down. Aces count as 1 or 11, face cards (King, Queen, Jack) count as 10, and the remaining cards count according to their pip value (for example, the 5 of Spades counts 5). A player is considered to have blackjack when he gets 21 with his first two cards. Blackjack beats 21. If the sum of the player's cards is closer to 21 than the dealer's he will win as much as he has put at stake. (If you bet $10 and win, you win $10.) If the player gets blackjack then he wins 1½ times the bet. (If you bet $10, you win $15.)

If the player's sum of cards is over 21 he loses, but if the player and the dealer have the same score from 17 or above, no one wins, and what the player bet goes back to the player. This is called a push. If the dealer gets blackjack against your blackjack, this will constitute a push.

Definitions and Rules

Blackjack Originally, any black Ace with a black Jack. Now an original hand containing an Ace and a 10-value card (10, Jack, Queen, or King) totaling 21. Pays 3–2.

Broke or Bust Going over 21 with additional cards drawn to the original hand.

Double Down Double down is done when the player thinks that the third card he is dealt will provide him with enough points to beat the dealer. If this is the case, the player will double his bet. You can double down after the first two cards are dealt, limiting your draw to only one more card.

Hard Total A hand with no Aces or where the Ace is counted as 1. Example, a King, 9 counts as a hard 19.

Hit or Draw Adding cards to your hand. You indicate that you want a hit by tapping the table with your forefinger or sweeping your fingers on the table toward you.

Insurance If the dealer's first card is an Ace then the player can, if he thinks the dealer's next card is a 10, insure himself against blackjack. To insure yourself against blackjack, it will cost you half your bet, but if the dealer gets blackjack it pays 2 to 1, which is the amount of your original bet. If you insure the hand and the dealer does not get blackjack then you lose your insurance. Insurance is considered as a game of its own within blackjack, and gives the player the chance to protect himself when he thinks the dealer has blackjack. The player should not insure himself when he has blackjack.

Natural A blackjack dealt with the original two cards.

Push You tie the dealer. Neither of you wins.

Soft Total A hand with an Ace that counts as an 11. Example, an Ace, 9 counts as a soft 20.

Split If the player is dealt the first two cards and they are of the same value, then he may split the hands (for example, Queen, 10 can be split or 8, 8). The player now has two separate hands, puts up a new stake and draws for both hands according to regular rules. If a player splits on two Aces, he will only be dealt one additional card on each hand. After these two cards are dealt, then the dealer draws his cards. If the player splits on two Aces and gets 21 on either hand, this is not considered blackjack, but 21.

Stand You like your hand as it is. Place your cards under your bet face down or give the proper hand signal (hand flat out, palm down, and move it side to side) to let the dealer know you don't want to hit.

Stiff Any hand that could "bust" by adding one more card; for example, a hard 12–16.

Upcard The face up card in the dealer's original hand.

Tips

The rules I have provided are those generally followed in all casinos; however, *every casino has its own house rules* that will vary slightly from the Vegas Strip Rules. These house rules are usually posted on a placard next to the blackjack table. If you don't see the rules—ask someone (a casino employee, not another player).

The minimum bet and the maximum bet (table limit) are posted. If you want to bet more than the table limit, the dealer needs to get permission from the pit boss who supervises a sector of tables. You will never be allowed to bet less than the minimum. If your bets suddenly jump up in value, the dealer will alert the floorperson or pit boss. You can be asked to leave the casino—even if you haven't broken any rules. If you are asked to leave, don't argue, just go to another casino. Casinos like to discourage steady winners.

To avoid soiling the cards (and the possibility of marking them), many casinos do not let you pick up your cards, but will deal both face up. In these casinos, you do not put your chips on the cards to indicate that you will stand; you use a hand signal (hand flat out, palm down, and move it side to side). No matter what casino you are in, the dealer will never react to a voice command but only to a hand signal (that is because everything at the table is on camera and it must be clear to his supervisors that there is no collusion between the dealer and player).

Standing

- Stand on all totals of 17 or higher.
- Stand on all totals of 13 or higher if the dealer is showing a 2 through 6.
- Always stand on a soft 19 and 20. (That's Ace, 8 or Ace, 9.)
- Always stand on Ace, 10. (That's because you've got blackjack!)
- Always stand on a pair of 10s.

When Should You Hit?

- Hit all totals of 12 to 16, provided the dealer is showing a 7 through Ace.
- Always hit all totals of 5 through 8.
- Always hit soft 13 through soft 17 if the dealer is showing 7 through Ace.

When Should You Split Pairs?

- Always split pairs of Aces and 8s.
- Never Split pairs of 4s, 5s, or 10s.
- Split other pairs depending whether the dealer's up card is weak or strong. The same goes for doubling down!

Should You Take Insurance?

Insurance should be used in certain situations, but as a beginning player you should almost never take insurance. Taking insurance usually favors the house.

56

Chess

The best way I can describe the game of chess is to compare it to broccoli. (Huh?) Now, if you are asking yourself, "Why broccoli?" Well, it is because I used to hate broccoli just as much as I hated chess, and the reason I hated them both was the same—I'd never tried them before. When I was about ten or so I was forced to eat broccoli casserole because we were at my uncle's house the night before Christmas and my mom said that Santa wouldn't bring me the G.I. Joe with the Kung Fu grip if I didn't eat every-thing on my plate. Guess what? I have *liked* broccoli ever since (unlike George Bush).

I also had the same experience with the game of chess. I always thought chess was a pain in the ass and thought it would be a rather boring game, but once again, I learned the hard way that all I had to do was try. I first played chess with a friend of mine in college; he was one of my fraternity brothers who you would never think even knew what chess was because it didn't involve drinking beer. However, he showed me how to play one night when we were supposed to be studying for mid-term exams (while drinking beer). Just like broccoli, I have liked the game of chess ever since.

Chess has been around for hundreds of years and is pretty much a uni-versal game. It is played in Asia, Europe, the Middle East, Australia, every-where. Chess is known as the game of the kings and is actually pretty easy to play once you learn a few simple rules.

Step 1. Preparing to Play

In almost all competitive games there is a way of determining who goes first. In chess one player holds a Black Pawn in one fist and a White Pawn in the other fist. The other player then chooses a hand, and whatever color Pawn is in that hand will be the color that that person plays. When playing chess *White* always makes the first move.

Step 2. Setting Up the Board

Setting up the chess pieces is rather easy. First make sure the board is prop-erly placed; the row of squares nearest to you should end in a *white* square on your *right*. All you have to remember is that the pieces get shorter as they move away from the King and Queen. The easiest way to set up is to first put the King and Queen on the board in the last row closest to you. The Kings are always facing each other along the same center vertical line and the Queen always goes on "her" color (White Queen on the center white square). Next to the Queen and the King go the Bishop, then the

Knight, then the Rook or Castle, then the Pawns in the next row in front. Just so you know, the horizontal rows of spaces are called the rank and the vertical rows of spaces are called the file. Rank and file, remember that.

Step 3. Game Pieces

King The King is the piece that both sides are trying to capture. The King can move one space in any direction.

Queen The Queen is like the King in the sense that it can move in any direction, but she can also move as many spaces as you want just as long as there is nothing blocking her path. The Queen is considered the most powerful piece on the board (just like in real life).

Bishop The Bishop can only move diagonally along its own color square, but any number of unobstructed spaces either forward or backward. Each side has a Bishop that moves along the black squares and one that moves along the white.

Rook The Rook or Castle can be moved forward, backward, or sideways any number of unobstructed spaces.

Knight This piece has the moving pattern that is the most confusing. The Knight moves one space forward, backward, or sideways and *then* it moves two spaces ahead. The Knight can also "jump" over other pieces. The jumped pieces are not captured, but if there is an opponent's piece on the square where the Knight is headed, it is captured.

Pawn The Pawn can move one space *forward* only except on its first move then it can move either one or two spaces. However, when it is capturing another piece it must move *diagonally* forward.

Step 4. Playing the Game

The Basics

The player who has selected the White playing pieces goes first, and the object of the game is to capture the King. The first move can either be moving a Pawn one or two spaces or moving a Knight. It is then Black's turn, and play then alternates between the two sides. In its simplest form, that is essentially how chess is played. The reason why a lot of people think it is a complicated game is because there are so many different types and combinations of moves that each player can make.

Additional Rules

1. The first time a Pawn is moved it can be moved one or two spaces. However, once it is moved for the first time, either one or two spaces, it can only move one space at a time.

2. When a Pawn has moved all the way to the other side of the board (to the last rank), it has to be replaced by a game piece of that player's choice. The Pawn can be "promoted" to any playing piece except a King. It is possible to have several promotions, and play with multiple Queens.

3. A game piece is "captured" when the player's game piece moves into a square occupied by a game piece of the opponent. The captured pieces are removed from the board. Only one piece can occupy a square at a time.

4. The only game piece that can "jump" is the Knight.

5. If a Pawn is moved to the fifth or sixth rank on the board and the other player moves a Pawn out two spaces in an adjacent column, the first player's Pawn can move behind the opposing Pawn, and declare an "en passant" capture (in passing). The Pawn is then removed from the board.

6. There is one time that a player can move two game pieces at once. Castling is when the King is moved either two spaces to the right or left and the Rook that the King has moved toward is moved to the space next to the King on the opposite side (the Castle jumps over the King). Castling can't be done if either the Rook or the King has been previously moved. It also can't be done if there are any other game pieces in between the Rook and King or if the King is in check.

Check, Checkmate, and Ending the Game

If one player is in a position so that his next move he could capture the other player's King, he says, "check." Saying check lets the other player know that his King is about to be captured. The player who has had check called on his King can either move the King, move another piece in between the threatening piece, or the threatening game piece can be captured. If the King can't move or get out of check, "checkmate" is called and the game is over. When checkmate is called, the King is not removed from the chess board, but it is laid down on its side on the game board. If the only move left for a King is into a position that would cause it to be in "check" then that move cannot be made. If he has no other pieces to move then the game is ended in a "stalemate" or a draw game. A player can never move his King into a check position. Often, if a player is ahead many pieces, an opponent may concede the game because the outcome is inevitable. Another way to end the game is to offer the opponent a draw and the game will end in a tie if he accepts.

PART SEVEN

Don't Try This at Home!
A Crash Course in Emergency First Aid

57

How to Perform the Heimlich Maneuver

As I am sure you can imagine, choking is a very scary thing for both the person who is choking, as well as, the people in the company of that person. If a person is choking, you should not interfere as long as he is *coughing*. Coughing means that the victim's air passage is not blocked and he can still force air in and out of his lungs. A person who is choking will either clasp or point at their neck instinctively. (As I am sure you can understand grasping your neck is considered the universal sign for choking.) Choking occurs when something goes down the windpipe rather than the food passage (esophagus), and the airway is partially or totally blocked. The Heimlich maneuver forces air out of the lungs to clear the blocking object. Quick action is essential when someone is choking. Brain death can occur in 4–6 minutes.

Step 1. Determine if the Person Is Choking

If someone is choking the victim's breathing will be extremely difficult, or they will be unable to cough or speak. The best way to help is to first ask, *"Are you choking?"* A choking victim can nod his head "yes," but will be unable to talk. At this time you have to take swift action. The reason it is important to *ask* if someone is choking is because a person suffering from a heart attack can have similar symptoms. Determine what is wrong before you act.

Step 2. The Abdominal Thrust

1. Stand behind the person with your arms around their waist.
2. Clench your fist and place it with the knuckle of the thumb against the victim's midsection, slightly above the navel but below the breastbone.
3. Hold your fist firmly with the other hand, bend your elbows, and pull both hands sharply toward you with an upward-and-inward motion.
4. This procedure should be administered continually until the object is forced out. If the object cannot be forced out in less than 15 seconds, have someone else call an ambulance. Continue the abdominal thrusts. It is possible that the victim may lose

consciousness. Don't worry about breaking a rib or injuring the person, if you don't dislodge what is choking them then they could choke to death. Perform abdominal thrusts as hard as you can.

If the Choking Person Loses Consciousness

1. Place them on their back on a level surface.
2. Take your index finger and use it like a hook to remove anything in the person's mouth that could block the air passage, but *be careful not to jam it any deeper into the windpipe.* (*Don't* do this to children or infants unless you can actually see the blocking object.)
3. Tilt the person's head back and lift the chin, pinch the nose closed, and put your mouth over the victim's, sealing the air passage. Blow two slow full breaths into the victim's air passage.
4. If the victim doesn't revive, put his legs together and straddle across the thighs. Put the heel of your dominant hand in his midsection just above the navel and put your other hand on top of it.
5. Straighten your arms out and quickly press the abdomen upward and inward. Repeat this until the blocked object is expelled. If the object doesn't come out in five to ten thrusts, repeat number 2 and 3, and then repeat the thrusts to the abdomen. (*Don't* administer abdominal thrusts to an *infant.* Anyone over a year old is OK.)

Pregnant or Overweight Person

1. Place them on their back on a level surface.
2. Put the legs together and straddle across the thighs. Place your hands on top of the *breastbone (sternum) in the middle of the chest* and rapidly press the chest until it compresses 1–1½ inches.
3. If they lose consciousness, follow the above procedure for finger sweeps and full deep breaths.

Infants (Children Under a Year Old)

1. Have someone call 911 or other medical help.
2. If the infant is conscious, sit down. Place the infant face down and straddle its legs over your forearm. Support the infant's weight with your thigh and support the throat and head with your hand. Keep the head lower than the body. Rapidly strike the infant on the back four or five times with the heel of your hand between the infant's shoulder blades.
3. If that doesn't dislodge the object, turn the infant over *supporting the neck and head.* Keep the head lower than the body. When the infant is turned onto its back use two or three fingers to deliver four or five thrusts to the breastbone (just below and between the

nipples), depressing the chest ½–1 inch. *Don't hit the ribs or the bottom of the sternum.*

4. Repeat numbers 2 and 3 until the object dislodges.
5. If the infant becomes unconscious, look into its mouth for the blocking object. Use a finger sweep *only if you can actually see* the object.
6. Tilt the head back and lift the chin. Pinch the nose shut and put your mouth over the infant's sealing the air passage. Blow two slow deep breaths into the infant.
7. Repeat the back blows and chest thrusts (remember to support the infant's head and neck at all times).
8. Repeat sequence of slow breaths, back blows, and chest thrusts until the object is dislodged or medical help arrives.

If You Are Alone and Choking

Believe it or not, you can perform the Heimlich maneuver on yourself! If there is someone else around, go to them immediately. If not:

1. First, don't panic. You have about three minutes before you will black out. Call 911; even if you can't talk, they can trace your phone call. Tap out SOS (three short taps, three long taps, three short taps) if you can. Leave the phone off the hook, the door open, and perform the maneuver on yourself.
2. Put your clenched fist a couple of inches above your navel with your thumb against your midsection. Grab it with your other hand and thrust upward and inward as hard as you can.
3. If this does not dislodge the blocking object, find some piece of furniture or architectural outcrop (the back of a hard chair, a staircase railing, a kitchen counter top, a newel post, etc.) and thrust yourself into it just above your navel. If you have to, run a few steps and then thrust yourself at the outcrop. Repeat or die.

Since its introduction, the Heimlich maneuver has saved over 60,000 lives. The next one could be you or someone you love.

58

How to Administer CPR

CPR, or cardiopulmonary resuscitation is a complex first aid procedure that is used on a person who is *not breathing* and has no heartbeat. Even though the following is a complete description of CPR, it is not intended as a substitute for a course that allows you to have actual hands-on experience. To learn CPR contact your local American Red Cross or American Heart Association to find out when classes are held. Statistics show that CPR is most often used by family members on each other, so it's a good idea that you know how to do it properly. In an emergency, however, even imperfect CPR is better than no CPR.

Step 1. Check for Consciousness and Call for Help

- Find out if the person is conscious, the best way is to *yell* "Are you OK? Can you breathe?" Tap them and yell again.
- If the person does not respond, call 911, then begin CPR.
- Do not try to move the person if it is not necessary. If they are not breathing, gently roll the person over onto their back, keeping the head, neck, and shoulders together as a unit. If you think that there may be a spinal injury, be careful to not move the person's neck unnecessarily.

Step 2. Check for Breathing

- The best way to check to see if a person is breathing is to put your cheek next to the person's mouth. If the person is breathing you should be able to feel the warm air on your face. Also, observe the person's chest and abdomen. If the person is breathing then there will be movement in that area.
- If there is vomit or some type of fluid in the mouth, clean out as much as possible with your fingers. Check the mouth, chest and abdomen again for movement. Sometimes clearing the mouth and airway is enough to get the person breathing again.
- If the person does not begin to breath immediately begin rescue breathing.

Step 3. Rescue Breathing

- After clearing the airway, push down and back on the forehead and lift up the chin. If the person is an infant, be careful not to tilt the head back too far, as it is possible to shut off the airway or damage the spine.
- Pinch the nostrils shut with your thumb and forefinger.
- Put your mouth over the other person's mouth, making sure there is a tight seal.
- Slowly blow air until the person's chest rises. Do this twice. Remove your mouth between breaths to allow the air to exhale the lungs.

Step 4. Check the Pulse

- Locate the main (carotid) artery in the neck by placing the tips of your index and middle finger on the Adam's apple and sliding them upward and back into the groove between the windpipe (trachea) and the muscles at the side of the neck. If the person is an infant check for the pulse at the inside of the upper arm (brachial pulse).
- Hold your fingers in place for 10 seconds.

If There Is a Pulse—*Do not do chest compressions on a person who has a pulse. This can cause serious injury.*

- Blow air into the lungs once every 5 seconds for an adult, and once every 4 seconds for a small child, and once every 3 seconds for an infant.
- Check the pulse once every 30 seconds to make sure the heart is still beating, and continue ventilating until the paramedics arrive.

If There Is No Pulse—Go to Step 5.

Step 5. Chest Compressions

- Run your fingers up the inside of the rib cage to the notch where the ribs meet the lower breastbone. It will be in the center of the lower part of the chest.
- Place the heel of one hand on the breastbone and your other hand on top, interlocking fingers. If the person is a small child, only use the heel of one hand. The heel of the hand is used for chest compression because if the fingers are used, it can damage the ribs and rib cage.
- Lock your elbows in place with your arms straight. Place your shoulders directly over your hands, so that the thrust of each compression goes straight down on the chest.
- Compress the chest 1–2 inches for an adult, pushing down with a firm and steady thrust. For a small child compress the chest 1–1½ inches.
- Without removing your hands from their position, lift your weight off the person's chest and repeat.
- After fifteen compressions, tilt the head, lift the chin (Step 3), pinch the nose, and blow two slow breaths. Make sure the chest deflates after each breath.
- Continue the cycle of fifteen compressions and two breaths. Check the person's pulse every minute.
- Continue until help arrives.

Chest Compressions on an Infant
- Place your index and middle fingers on the baby's breastbone and gently compress the chest no more than 1 inch. Count out loud as you pump, about one compression per 1–1½ seconds.
- Give one breath after every fifth compression.

Step 6. Take a Class
- After you have finished reading these directions go sign up immediately for a CPR class.

59

How to Treat Exposure to Temperature Extremes

Hypothermia

Hypothermia is when your body heat is lost faster than it can be produced and the body temperature drops below 95°F. This condition can develop quickly and become serious with almost no warning.

Symptoms

Cold skin, shivering, dizziness, confusion, slurred speech, staggering, unresponsiveness to pain or verbal stimulus, and slow pulse or breathing. As the body's temperature continues to drop the person can slip into unconsciousness and his breathing and pulse can stop. If breathing or pulse stops, administer CPR.

What to Do

1. Get to a warm dry place.
2. Remove any wet clothing.
3. Rewarm the person slowly by direct application of external heat to both sides of the victim's trunk (skin to skin contact from two rescuers is the best method), making sure you keep the victim awake.
4. Give warm liquids and high calorie foods.
5. Do *not* give alcohol. (It dilates the blood vessels, causing them to lose heat faster.)

Frostbite

Frostbite is the actual freezing of the skin or the tissues near the surface of the skin. Frostbite can occur even if the temperature is not below freezing, but other weather conditions, such as rain and wind, cause the skin to freeze. Frostbite occurs most commonly in the elderly and small children.

Symptoms

The initial symptoms of frostbite are that the area feels numb and tingly. It will begin to turn white, and as the skin freezes it will become hard. In severe frostbite cases, the skin will look black, blue, and white, and the area is very cold and hard.

What to Do?

1. In cases of frostbite, rewarm as quickly as possible. Put the frostbitten body parts in water of 104°F to 108°F for 15–20 minutes.
2. Do *not* rub or massage the frozen area.
3. Do not break any blisters that have formed.
4. You may want to give the person aspirin or Tylenol to fight the burning sensation associated with frostbite.
5. Attempt to rewarm only if you are sure that you are in a place where refreezing will not occur.
6. Watch for signs of infection, and *see a doctor*. These signs of infection may occur 24–48 hours after frostbite:
   - Redness, or red streaks in the infected area
   - Swelling
   - Tenderness
   - Pus
   - Fever of 101°F or higher
   - Swollen lymph nodes

Heat Exhaustion

Heat exhaustion occurs when your body can't cool off and maintain a comfortable body temperature. Hot temperatures, exercise, and dehydration can cause the body to overheat. People who are at risk include the elderly, small children, people who overexert themselves, and people who work outside.

Symptoms

1. Weakness
2. Headache

3. Fatigue
4. Nausea
5. Dizziness
6. Muscle cramps
7. Shallow breathing

What to Do

1. Move to a cool place in the shade or into an air-conditioned room.
2. Remain quiet.
3. Loosen clothing.
4. If you are dizzy, lie down with your head lower than your feet.
5. Drink small amounts of liquid, every 15 minutes. Don't gulp down a large amount at one time. If you do, it will make you vomit.
6. Place a cool wet cloth on your forehead.
7. Do *not* consume alcohol.
8. Watch for heat stroke.

Heat Stroke

Heat stroke is the final stage of heat exhaustion, and is considered a medical emergency. The body's cooling system is considered overloaded when temperature reaches 104°F, and the temperature continues to rise.

Symptoms

- Hot dry skin
- Flushed or bright red skin
- Body temperature of 105°F or greater
- Disorientation, delirium, unconsciousness
- Constricted pupils
- Deep rapid breathing followed by shallow or absent breathing
- Fast and weak pulses

If someone is suspected of having a heat stroke, call 911 immediately. While waiting for help, give a cold water bath, sponge the person's body with cool water, or apply cool wet sheets. Monitor the person's body temperature every ten minutes. Stop trying to cool the person if their temperature drops rapidly and signs of shock develop.

60

How to Treat Shock

What Is Shock?

When your vital organs can't get the blood and oxygen they need, your body will go into shock. Shock should always be considered an emergency, and assistance should be called immediately. Several different conditions can cause your body to go into shock: bleeding, pain, a high or low body temperature, poisoning, severe illness, or an allergic reaction.

Signs of Shock

1. Pale, clammy skin
2. Weak, rapid pulse
3. Shallow, rapid breathing
4. Confusion or anxiety
5. Dizziness, weakness, or loss of consciousness
6. Dilated pupils
7. Nausea or vomiting
8. Thirst

What to Do?

- If you suspect that someone has gone into shock, it is extremely important that you act immediately. Don't wait to see whether the person improves.
- Call 911 or a local emergency service.
- While you are waiting, have the person lie down and elevate the legs higher than the heart. If you suspect a head or neck injury, keep the person flat. Do not attempt to move him.
- If the person has vomited, roll him onto his side and try to drain his mouth.
- If the person is bleeding, apply direct pressure.
- Keep the person warm, unless the shock is due to heat stroke.
- Do not give the person anything to eat or drink.
- Take and keep a record of the person's pulse. (Feel for a pulse on the person's wrist, and count the number of beats in 15 seconds, them multiply by four. This will give the heartbeats per minute.)

61

How to Control Severe Bleeding

Call 911 or emergency services and while you are waiting for help to arrive:

- Have the injured person lie down with their head slightly lower than their body. Try to elevate the legs and the site of the bleeding.
- Keep the person warm, to lessen the possibility of shock.
- *Do not* try to clean the wound. However, if it can be easily done, remove any large pieces of debris and dirt.
- Place a clean cloth over the wound and apply direct steady pressure for 15 minutes. Use your bare hands only if necessary.
- *Do not* apply direct pressure if there is an object in the wound or a bone is protruding. If a broken bone is involved, apply pressure around the wound.
- If the bleeding has not stopped after 15 minutes and help has still not arrived, apply firm continuous pressure on a pressure point between the wound and the heart. This will restrict blood flow through the major arteries, helping to slow the bleeding. Apply pressure to pressure points, which are located on the inside upper arms and on the upper thighs in the groin area.
- In severe cases of bleeding, when other methods have failed, and a limb is partially or wholly severed, you can apply a tourniquet. A strap, belt, towel, or other item that can be used to apply pressure can be used as a tourniquet. Apply it above the wound and between the wound and the heart. Wrap the tourniquet twice around the limb and tie a half-hitch knot on the top. Place a short stick on the half-hitch and secure it with a square knot. Twist the stick to tighten until the bleeding is controlled.

62

How to Treat Burns

What is the body's largest organ? Believe it or not, the skin. Our skin protects us from infection, helps to regulate our temperature, and keeps our balance of water in check. Any injury that interferes with those vital processes can be fatal. Burns either caused by fire, hot liquids, electricity, chemicals, and even radiation are the type of injury that are the most likely to affect a large area of our skin. Burns are classified by the depth of their penetration of the skin.

First Degree Burns These burns only affect the tougher, outer layer of skin. The skin turns bright red and becomes sensitive and painful. It will be dry, it will not blister, but it may swell.

Second Degree Burns These burns are deeper than first degree burns. They are very painful, red, and splotchy. The area may blister and be puffy and swollen.

Third Degree Burns These burns are very deep and can affect the skin, muscle, bone, and internal organs. The skin will look dry, charred, and even black. The underlying muscles or tendons may be visible. If the nerves have been damaged, there will be no pain except around the edges of the burn, but if there is no nerve damage, pain will be excruciating.

What to Do for Severe Burns

- The first thing to do is to call for help. After that, check to see that the person is breathing. If not, start CPR.
- If there is severe bleeding, get it under control.
- Signs of shock: paleness, faintness, rapid and weak pulse, shallow breathing, cool, clammy skin.
- With burn damage around the mouth and nose, there may be damage in the respiratory tract that needs immediate emergency care.

If You Are on Fire

- If you are on fire, you have to remember the key words: *stop, drop, and roll.* Rolling on the ground will smother and put out the flames. Whatever you do, don't go running around, it will only cause the fire to burn more intensely.
- If someone else is on fire, help them to stop, drop, and roll, and try to smother the flames with a blanket, rug, or coat. Don't let them run around, because, well, they are on fire.
- Make sure the fire is completely extinguished, by soaking with water. *Do not* remove any burned clothing at this time. Call 911.
- Cover the burn with a dry sterile bandage or a clean, dry sheet.

Electrical Burns

- Turn off the power before touching someone who is in contact with an electrical wire.

- Assume any electrical wire is live.
- If it is possible, do not move the person.
- If a power line has fallen across a car, the people, if not in immediate danger, will be safer in the car until help arrives.
- Monitor for shock and apply CPR if the victim is not breathing.
- Electrical burns can seem minor, even when there have been major injuries. Any electrical burns should be evaluated by a doctor.

Chemical Burns

- Flush the skin for twenty minutes with a lot of cool running water. If the chemical is dry, brush it off first.
- If chemicals have burned an eye, flush it immediately with lukewarm water. Make sure you angle the head of the person so that when you are flushing the contaminated eye, the contaminant does not flow into the other eye. Cover with a loose dressing and see a doctor.
- Remove any contaminated clothing or jewelry.
- Cover the affected area with a cool, damp, sterile cloth (if you have one) and see a doctor.
- Keep the victim warm and monitor for shock until medical help arrives.

63

How to Treat a Nosebleed

The nose has a hard bony part near where it attaches to your face and a soft part, made of cartilage, approximately in the middle of your nose. A nosebleed occurs when one or more of the blood vessels at the upper end of the soft part is damaged. Some common causes of nosebleeds are: picking your nose too much, constantly rubbing your nose, blowing your nose or sneezing frequently during a cold or an attack of hay fever, or, the ever popular, getting hit in the nose.

Step 1. Lean Your Head Forward

Contrary to common belief the best thing to do is to lean your head forward, not back like many people believe, and let the blood drain out of your nose and not down your throat. Sit down and loosen the clothes around your neck. Try to breathe through your mouth normally.

Step 2. Hold Your Nose

While leaning your head forward, squeeze the nose firmly just below the hard part (basically right in the middle). Hold it there for about 5 minutes. You may want to put some tissue, or cotton up your nostrils to catch the blood. Release after 5 minutes to check if bleeding has stopped, and if it has not, squeeze it again for another 5 minutes. After the bleeding has stopped, try to continue to breathe through your mouth. Do not blow your nose or try to clear any blood clots for about 3 hours. If your nose continues to bleed it is best to see a doctor.

PART EIGHT

Goin' to the Chapel:
A Crash Course in Wedding Etiquette

64

How to Get Engaged

Getting married is probably the biggest single decision that you will make in your life. If you screw up and marry the wrong person, you will either be miserable for the rest of your life or you will get a divorce and have to give her half of your stuff. You don't want to mess this one up. I don't know every custom or requirement, but I believe there are three rules for getting married. They are very basic. Even though they won't predict that the marriage will last, they will help you with your decision.

Rule Number 1. Do You Really Want to Do This?

Don't get married because your parents really like her or because she is the best looking thing this side of the race track or because she can cook really well. Marry her because she is your best friend and you would do anything for her. Again, I don't know if there are any definitive answers or rules for getting engaged, but I have developed my own set of rules that may help you decide if *you* want to marry your girlfriend. I told a friend of mine what I am about to tell you and no less than a week later he was engaged to his girlfriend of four years.

1. *Show me the hottest girl in the world and I will show you the guy who is tired of having sex with her.* It helps to know your girlfriend on an almost daily basis for *two years* prior to getting married. The initial glow of love can fade *real* fast. No matter what you do, you are going to get older, and as you will find out for yourself, sex and looks are a lot less important than they seem now. The last thing I want is to be married to an absolute babe who is an absolute pain in the ass. For example, Cindy Crawford and Richard Gere, they were a very attractive couple, but they didn't have what it takes to make it for the long haul.

2. *If you walk out the front door, get hit by a bus, and become a quadriplegic do you think your girlfriend would stay by your side?* If you think that your girlfriend will stick around to wipe your butt, feed you creamed vegetables all day, and put up with your crap; and you honestly believe that the answer is "yes" to this question, then marry her.

3. *If your girlfriend walks out the front door, gets hit by a bus, and becomes a quadriplegic, do you think you would stay?* I know that is a difficult thought, but you have to be ready for the unexpected. Statistics say that one in five people will become disabled in their lifetime. Hoping and praying that you or your beautiful wife will not be one of those five people is not going to cut it.

I know that those seem like some pretty basic suggestions to help find the answer to a very big question, but just like my seventh grade science teacher said, "The answer was right in front of you the whole time."

Rule Number 2. Does She Really Want to Do This?

Never, and I mean never, ask a woman to marry you if you have any doubt about the answer you will receive. I have seen rejection reduce the strongest of men to empty hollowed shells, left to rot in their own self-inflicted despair and loneliness. Unfortunately, the only person who can answer this question would be your future Mrs. Before you do anything drastic, the best thing to do is to try to put some feelers out. Try to get an understanding of what she is thinking by dropping a few strong hints here and there. This may sound like an extreme suggestion, but it works well if used properly. One day, in a casual atmosphere, when she is least expecting it say "Do you think you would ever want to get married?" (Read on before you form an opinion.) I like this tactic because it is so direct, yet you can play it off, based on how she answers. Here is an example: You are in the drive-through at Taco Bell, you have just placed an order, and are sitting in your car discussing the pros and cons of hitchhiking, when you can slip in your question. If she gets mushy and says "Of course," then you have nothing to worry about, but if she looks at you like you are crazy, then you can blow it off by saying something like, "Some guy at work got married the other day, and I don't think I am ready just yet, and for some reason Taco Bell reminded me of him." Then your food will be ready and you can drive away. The downside to this plan is that it can easily backfire, so you have to be able to think on your feet. Your girlfriend will undoubtedly ask twenty questions about the guy who got married so be ready to make up some more crap to throw her off. You might also try asking a trusted girlfriend of hers what she thinks about your relationship before you drop any hints about marriage.

Rule Number 3. Ask Her Parents

This is more of a common courtesy to ask the permission of the father prior to asking the future bride. More than anything else, it is rude if you don't. Also, you may be putting her parents into a position where they have to spend a lot of money on a wedding. You don't want to drop that in the father's lap without giving him some idea of what he is in for. Believe me, he will not be happy.

This is not the eighteenth century so, it is perfectly acceptable to ask both parents, or the mother of the bride if that is appropriate to the situation. Offer to take them to lunch or dinner, but if you decide to take this route ask them prior to eating. They probably know why you are there so it is best to lay all your cards on the table and get it out in the open. This way everyone can enjoy their food and relax.

I hope you didn't think that these few paragraphs would provide you with an easy solution to a big decision. Just take my words of advice and use them to guide you along the way to making your own decisions. This is one of those things you are going to have to decide for yourself. Remember, marriage is a *contract* between two people for sharing economic and emotional needs. It is not love, not children, and not sex (you can have all of those without marriage) although marriage can and does contain all three. Just be *sure* before you ask. If you have *any* hesitation, wait and see how things develop, *then* act.

65

How to Pick Out a Diamond

When you get engaged, you will need an engagement ring—a diamond engagement ring, because diamonds are forever (hopefully, so will your marriage). Diamonds are formed between 75 and 120 miles below the earth's surface, and are made of pure carbon. The carbon crystallizes under intense heat and pressure and were originally sent to the surface of the earth by volcanic eruptions. Now we just dig for them.

Ever heard of the saying "size doesn't matter"? Well, when it comes to women that phrase doesn't apply. However, to a gemologist that is only part of the equation. A relative of mine had a diamond reappraised for insurance purposes and because the diamond had a scratch, that couldn't be seen by the naked eye, it was appraised at a value less than what it was ten years ago. *Be careful* when buying a diamond. There is a lot more than size that matters.

To establish the relative value of any gem, it is necessary to evaluate the color, clarity, cut, and carat weight. The "4Cs." *The terminology used in the following definitions is in accordance with the gemological institute of America (GIA).*

Diamond Terminology

1. **Shape** It refers to the actual shape or outline of the stone. (Round, brilliant, pear, emerald, oval, heart, etc.) Shape is not the same as cut.

2. **Cut** The cut of the diamond is what determines the amount of light reflected. These cuts form angled flat surfaces and are called *facets*. For example, a round (shape) and brilliant (cut) diamond has 58 facets, or angled surfaces. The better the cut of the diamond, the greater the ability of the diamond to reflect light (brilliance). The cut directly affects the diamond's brilliance and as a result its value.

3. **Measurements** These are the dimensions of the stone in millimeters. Depth (table to culet) and diameter (across girdle).

4. **Carat Weight** Gems are weighed in units called carats. One carat is equal to one hundred points, or two hundred milligrams. A ¼ carat stone is therefore 0.25 ct. or 25 points. The word "carat" originated from the "carob" tree. Because the seeds of the carob tree were very consistent in weight, they were used by early gem traders to weigh their jewels.

5. **Clarity Grade** Diamonds have identifying marks called "inclusions." The less inclusions a diamond has, the better it is. If the appraisal is for a diamond, the stone is assigned one of the following clarity grades:

   Flawless Any stone that is free from all external and internal faults or blemishes under 10× power-corrected lens magnification, such as a binocular, dark-field diamond scope.

   VVS1-VVS2 Very, very slightly imperfect. These stones will have internal inclusions or surface blemishes, more numerous and easier to locate than the flawless grade under 10× magnification.

   VS1-VS2 Very slightly imperfect. These stones will have internal inclusions or surface blemishes, more numerous and easier to locate than the VVS1 grade under 10× magnification.

   SI1-SI2 Slightly imperfect. These stones have more serious inclusions and surface blemishes than the VS1-VS2 grade. However, these inclusions are not apparent with the naked eye when viewing the stone through the table.

   I1-I2-I3 Imperfect. These stones contain internal defects or surface blemishes that can be seen with the unaided eye.

6. **Color Grade** The best diamonds are considered colorless. Colorless diamonds allow white light to pass through, this gives

diamonds their rainbow effect. There are also diamonds that are colored, such as pink, blue, red, or green. During formation other elements, like nitrogen or boron, have been mixed in with the diamond's structure. This gives the diamond its color, or lack of it. In general D-G colors are more valuable than diamonds categorized as N-Z. (I don't know why they didn't use A, B, or C. I guess that was too easy.) If the appraisal is for a diamond, the stone will be given one of the following color grades:

D, E, F These stones are considered colorless.

G, H, I These stones will face up almost colorless, but will have some slight tint of color. Larger stones will seem to be more tinted than smaller stones.

J, K These stones will have a more tinted appearance than the former grades.

L, M, N, O These stones will display a yellowish tint even to the untrained eye.

P–X These stones continue to approach the darker yellow tint.

7. **Depth** Measured in a percentage. Ratio of depth to diameter measurements.
8. **Table Diameter** Percentage ratio of the table width to the stone diameter.
9. **Girdle Thickness** Percentage ratio of the girdle thickness to the total depth.
10. **Culet Size** The culet (facet at the bottom tip of the stone) should be as small as possible. Grade is related to the size in comparison to the size of the stone.
11. **Finish** This includes other aspects of the stone such as polish, symmetry, and girdle finish.

Which Should You Choose?

When a woman shows her friends a new diamond engagement ring, what do you think is the first thing that pops into her head, is it: (A) "Wow, that thing is huge" (or in most cases, "Wow, that thing is small"), or is it (B) "Wow, that diamond must be cut to ideal proportions, which allows for the maximum amount of light to reflect and refract, thus creating an astonishing brilliance, sparkle, and fire"?

I don't think I am going out on a limb here when I say that I can bet that in 99.99 percent of all women will be thinking answer "A." I bring this up because it is possible to buy a larger diamond that may have some imperfections that you couldn't tell with the naked eye. As a result, it is possible to purchase a bigger diamond for a cheaper price. On that same note, make sure you can find a reputable jeweler. Since a vast majority of the male population has no clue about diamonds, other than the size, it's easy for us to get ripped off.

66

How to Be a Best Man

If you ask a guy what his duties are if he is going to be the best man in a wedding, 99.99 percent will answer, "Throw a bachelor party." Being best man requires a lot more time and effort than just throwing a bachelor party, even though that is also a responsibility, it is not the only thing. Before you take on the responsibility of being a best man you have to make sure that you will have the time. Your friend has just basically asked you to be his assistant in one of the biggest events in his life. If your work requires you to be out of town a lot, or you live hours away, you may want to take this into consideration. Make sure you can be there for your friend. There are different types of weddings, some may be more formal than others or the groom's parents may do some of your work for you, but I wanted to try to provide you with every option so you can make sure all the bases are covered.

You Must Go to Parties and Functions

Depending upon the length of engagement, there may be several parties that you have to attend. Plan to attend engagement parties and showers thrown by friends and relatives. I knew one couple that had four different parties. Even the groom's father threw a groom's shower where we had to all buy tools as gifts. (Actually that was pretty cool. We just sat around and drank beer, ate pizza, and watched football.) When you are the best man in a wedding, don't worry about giving a gift at each party. (Unless you are loaded.) The fact that there will be a few different parties is taken into consideration, and as the best man it is expected that you are to purchase only one gift and give it to the bride and groom prior to, or after, the wedding at whatever function that you deem most appropriate.

You Must Throw a Bachelor Party

Previously, the traditional bachelor party was the night before the wedding, but I think people started to realize that the groom usually got pretty loaded and sometimes found it hard to make it to the wedding the next day. I heard a story once that a guy had a bachelor party on the Friday night before his wedding. He and his buddies went out to a few bars, and as luck would have it, they got a little too rowdy, got in a fight, and the groom was thrown in jail. I don't know if you know this, but where I am from if you are thrown in jail on Friday night you don't get out until Monday morning. Try to have the party at least a few days prior to the actual wedding. I think the tradition bylaws have been updated so that the bachelor party should be held on the weekend before the wedding. However, you may want to coordinate with the other guys in the wedding party before you make any concrete plans.

Talk to the groom prior to throwing the bachelor party and find out what he would prefer to do. Some brides tell their future husbands that if she finds out that there was any type of stripper at the party then the wedding is off. Don't be an idiot and talk to her directly, but ask the groom what her objections are, believe me, he will know. If you are going to turn your house into an amateur strip joint, make sure there is plenty of booze, snacks (just some chips and light stuff will be fine; it is hard to enjoy a lap dance on a stomach full of ribs), and that everyone has a safe ride home. If anyone gets in trouble it is *your* ass. Also, respect the fact that some guys don't like to get loaded and play "pin the tail on the stripper" either. If he just wants to go fishing or play golf with the guys, then that is fine. Coordinate accordingly.

You Must Give Speeches or Toasts

Speeches and toasts (there are some examples in the next chapter) are usually given at the rehearsal dinner (after the actual dinner) and at the wedding (prior to the cake being cut). However, there may also be other opportunities, like at a shower or party, so you may want to have a few different versions ready to be given at any time. Don't worry about writing a long drawn-out speech, just make sure you have something nice or funny to say. The speech or toast at the rehearsal dinner is usually longer and more sappy than the one at the actual wedding. Sometimes you are the only one giving a speech; sometimes others will follow you. You may want to tell a funny story about the groom and yourself. (However, don't overdo it and tell anything too embarrassing; any story that starts with, "I remember the time [*Insert groom's name here*] and I went to Amsterdam after we graduated college, and he smoked so much pot that . . .") Then say something nice about the bride, even if you don't mean it. Finally, say how happy you are to be involved with their special day. Bla, Bla, Bla.

The toast at the wedding usually comes before the cake is cut (but after the bar has opened so people will laugh at your jokes) and is best when kept short and sweet. Say something funny or emotional, but others also want to get on the mike so do keep it short.

You Are Responsible for the Tuxedos

Picking up the tuxes is usually the time that you begin to act as the ring-leader of the groom and the groomsmen. The groom will be a mess, and the groomsmen, usually old friends or relatives, will be screwing around. You have to make sure that the groom doesn't fall apart or the groomsmen don't give each other wedgies in the parking lot. As a best man it is your responsibility to pick up, but not necessarily pay for, the groom's tux. Make sure it is all there and also fits correctly. You also you have to return the tux after he has left for the honeymoon. (If you throw the groom into a pool, be prepared to pay a fine to the tuxedo rental shop.) Just to be safe, try to make sure the other groomsmen have gotten their tuxes and everything fits on them too.

On the Day of the Wedding

The day of the wedding you are the right-hand man of the groom. Your responsibilities include: doing what ever he wants you to, telling him that he is doing the right thing, keeping him occupied until it is time to go to the church, making sure he has the ring, and making sure he gets there *on time*. Treat this like going to the airport, get there at least an hour before the wedding. If you have to make the bride wait, no matter what happens, it will be *your* fault.

You Must Hold the Ring

Sometime prior to the ceremony, the groom will give you the wedding band that he is going to put on the bride's finger. Once it is in your possession it is your responsibility. I suggest that you get it from him no more than an hour before the ceremony. This way you will have less time to lose it. Also, check your pants pockets to see if you have any holes in them. Whatever you do, hold onto it for dear life.

After the Wedding

If the groom and bride have not already done so, make sure they have transportation to the reception. They usually will have a limo or some sort of transportation already lined up, but double check just to be sure.

If the bride and groom are driving to their honeymoon or to the airport, it is your responsibility to decorate the car they will be leaving in. Prior to the wedding, you may want to gather some string, some soda cans, toilet paper, condoms, shaving cream, etc. Decorate the car, as you see fit, but don't do anything that will endanger their lives. (For example: Don't remove all the lug nuts from the wheels, even though that would be pretty funny.) I recommend shaving cream over whipped cream because the sugar in whipped cream can harm a car's paint.

When you are decorating the car, it would be a good time to make sure they have all their luggage packed, in the car, and ready to go. Don't forget your final responsibility is getting the groom's tux back to the tuxedo rental store. Don't be late, those fines can be ridiculous.

Additional Responsibilities

1. Send flowers to the bride's mother the week before the wedding.
2. Offer to have out-of-town guests stay at your house if you have the space.
3. Offer your services to both the bride's and the groom's parents prior to the wedding. (For example, offer to pick up crazy Uncle Larry from the airport.)
4. If something has not been arranged prior to this time, take the gifts from the wedding reception (but don't keep them!).
5. Offer to take care of the bride's or groom's pets while they are away.

67

How to Give a Toast

It is very safe to say that if you ever have to give a serious toast it will be at a wedding, or some other special occasion that will strongly resemble a wedding. There are very few occasions that guys can say sappy things to, and in the company of, other guys and get away with it.

Let me provide you with an example. If Gary is Bob's best friend and at Bob's wedding to Sara, Gary gets up and says "Bob is my best friend, and I love him very much, I wish him the best of luck and I hope his life will continue to be as happy as I know he is today." Well, then all of Gary and Bob's other friends will consider that gesture a touching display of emotion. If Gary and Bob are at a basketball game and Gary gets up and says, "Bob is my best friend, and I love him very much, I wish him the best of luck and I hope his life will continue to be as happy as I know he is today," then people are going to question Bob and Gary's relationship, and the validity of Bob's marriage to Sara. Did you get all that?

There are no official rules for giving a toast, but I have put together some basic guidelines to follow for giving a toast.

Toasting Etiquette

Stand up if you are giving a toast and stay seated to receive one. If you are being toasted you do not raise your glass or drink when the others drink.

It is your job to sit there and hear your praise. You take a sip after everyone else has but *take a sip*; it is considered rude and a rejection of the toast if you don't drink.

Giving a Toast

Confidence is the key in good speech delivery, don't worry about what other people think, they want you to do a good job just as much as you do. Relax, you're among friends, and I bet a lot of people will be half-cocked anyway. What ever you do, do not read a toast from a piece of paper. If you know you are going to have to give a speech in advance it is best to write it out on paper and practice it. Practice it enough so that when you do give it, it is delivered without any major flubs. Once the big time comes, one of the most important things is that you need to be sure that everyone can hear you. Don't scream, but make sure you are speaking loud enough so that you can be heard. (If it is a toast at a wedding, then you may want to get another groomsman to stand at the back of the room so he can give you hand signals. He could tell you to speak up or quiet down, or tell you to stop rambling.) Make sure you don't speak too fast either. When you are practicing be conscious of your speed. Even though you will be a little nervous, try not to think about the fact that you are speaking to such a large group. Stand up straight and look at the audience. (Good posture helps to project your voice too.) Try to look around the room, making eye contact with a few people. Keep track of your thoughts, keep a huge smile on your face, act natural, and it will be over before you know it.

The Structure of a Toast

Here is a basic framework that can be used to prepare for any toast. If you are in a room where you don't know a lot of the guests, it is best to let the guests know who you are and why you are giving a toast. Retirement party example: My name is Pat McGroin and when I started working for Huge Company, Inc. Bob was the first person to . . .

Some of the best toasts are of a personal and humorous story about the person you are toasting. Remember toasts are supposed to be funny but not uncomfortable. Don't tell any "revealing" stories and keep it in good taste. Finally, the number-one rule when you are giving a toast is to keep it short and sweet. Long stories or toasts are annoying and the other guests will get bored quickly.

Sample Wedding Toasts

- Remember: Settle every argument before bedtime, praise quickly, criticize slowly, trust in your heart, believe in your fate, and always remember they were one hell of a date.

- As you slide down the banister of life, may all the splinters be pointing the right direction.
- The worst thing about being the best man is that you don't get to prove it!
- A toast to love and laughter, and happily ever after.
- I have four pieces of advice: Love each other; Talk to each other; Listen to each other; and Help each other. God bless your lives.
- May your worst day together be better than your best day apart.
- May your best of yesterdays be your worst of tomorrows.
- A marriage is kept healthy by lying, cheating, and stealing . . . Never lie to each other, never cheat on each other, but make sure you steal away plenty of time to be together.
- If love makes the world go around, you two should make it spin!
- As only one of your friends who have been married for at least (X) years I want to tell you that the road to that point is often bumpy but the journey is well worth it! Here's to love, life, and happiness!
- To a great fisherman and his best catch ever.
- May your love be modern enough to survive the times and old-fashioned enough to last forever.
- (*Bride*) and (*groom*): A case of love pure and simple (*bride*) is pure and (*groom*) is simple.
- When you shout, may you shout for joy. When you cry, may you cry tears of happiness. When you lie, may you lie in each other's arms. And when you fight, may you fight for love!
- May you add to each other's joys,
  Subtract from each other's sorrows,
  May your blessings be multiplied,
  But your hearts never divided.
- (*Bride*), put your left hand on the table. (*Groom*), put your hand over hers. (*Groom*), take a good, long look at this; it will be the last time you'll get the upper hand in anything!

Sample Non-Wedding Toasts

- To the Chef: Good food, good meat, good God, let's eat!
- Beer is proof that God loves us and wants us to be happy.
- May you be in heaven a half hour before the devil knows you're dead.
- Here is to the fools of the world . . . without them, the rest of us could not succeed.
- May we get what we want out of life and what we deserve out of life—and may they be the same thing!

- Fresh horses and beer for all the men for tonight we ride!
- Here's to those who wish us well! And all the rest can go to h—!
- May you live as long as you want to, and want to as long as you live. And may all of your ups and downs be between the sheets!
- Here's to wives and girlfriends and may they never meet!
- I'd rather be with the people here today, than with the nicest people in the world!
- Don't eat yellow snow!
- May the most you ever wish for be the least you ever receive.

PART NINE

There's No Place Like Home:
A Crash Course in Basic Home Ec

68

How to Sew On a Button

What I am not going to teach here is Home Economics 101. If you want to learn how to make a shirt or a stuffed animal, take a class. I am going to teach you how to sew on a button in less than five minutes, because buttons *will* come off at the most inconvenient times and chances are your mom won't be around to sew it back on.

What You Will Need
Needle and thread, or a small sewing kit.

Tip
If you don't have a needle and thread lying around, then I recommend keeping a small sewing kit for these inopportune moments. It is best to keep it with your travel gear so you know where it is, and if you travel, you will have it with you. A small sewing kit can be picked up at any local drugstore, and it will only cost a couple of bucks.

Step 1. Don't Panic
The first thing you need to do is look for your button. If you can't find the button in about ten seconds, don't worry about it. Almost all men's shirts, and some men's pants have a spare button sewn somewhere onto the fabric. (Spare buttons on dress shirts are usually located on the shirt tails, and spare buttons on pants are located on the inner lining, near the zipper.)

Step 2. Threading the Needle
After either locating the old button or removing the spare button, get your sewing kit and take a good look at it. You will probably find a few needles, and a few different types of thread; a more elaborate version will have small scissors, a wider variety of thread, some spare buttons, and possibly some safety pins. Once you have opened the kit, find the thread that most resembles the color of the thread of the button that you lost. It will probably be black or white.

Remove about three feet of thread and one of the larger needles from the kit. Make sure you don't pick a needle that is too big to fit through the holes of the button. Once you have the thread out, fold it in half and hold it at the point where you have folded it. This fold is to be threaded through the eye of the needle. You may have to lick the thread, or twist it, but what ever you do, just get it through the needle's eye. (A larger needle will have a larger eye, thus it will be a little easier to thread.)

Once you have threaded the needle, pull the thread half-way through, and fold the thread over again. Tie all four pieces of thread together in a small knot as close to the end as you can get it. This will leave you with, a knot at one end, a needle at the other, and four strands of thread about 7–8 inches long in between.

Quadrupling your thread enables you to quickly sew on the button. Every time you pull the needle through it will be as if you are doing it four times. This will dramatically cut the time you spend sewing.

Step 3. Emergency Surgery

Once you have the needle ready to go, find where the button was located on your shirt or pants. If there are any torn threads still there, cut or pull them away. Make sure the cloth is thread-free before you start. Starting from the back of the fabric, push the needle through one of the holes that was left behind from the previous button. Pull it all the way through, until it stops at the knot. Now take a look at your button. It will have a few holes in it, usually four, sometimes two; pick one and put the needle through it. Push the button down the needle and thread and against the fabric. Pull the thread tight, and bring it down back through the hole in the button that is *diagonal* to the hole in the button you initially put the needle and thread through. The goal is to create an "X" with the thread, not a square. The "X" pattern of the thread keeps the button secure, but also allows movement so you can actually get the button through the buttonhole. Now bring the needle back through the fabric and through a different hole in the button. Repeat two to three times.

Step 4. Finishing Up

When you are near the end of the thread, make sure that when you make your last pass you end up with the needle at the back of the fabric. At this point pass the needle through the stitches you have created in the back of the button two or three times. This should keep it securely in place. Cut off the remaining thread. Get dressed and go.

Tip

If the fabric you are sewing is very thick you will need to have some space in between the button and the garment in order for the buttonhole to catch properly. If this is the case, when you are sewing on the button, place a match or a toothpick in between the button and the fabric. When you are done sewing, it can be removed and should leave enough space for the buttonhole to catch properly.

69

How to Set a Table

Some people may think that how to set a table is common knowledge; however, you would be surprised at how many people don't know how to do it properly. I am going to show you two table settings, standard and formal. For each, you need to know that flatware is a set of matching knives, forks, and spoons, and a place setting is what goes on the table for each guest. It consists of flatware, plates, glasses, and the napkin.

Tips

1. Make sure your silverware, plates, and glasses are clean of spots and dust. Don't use a dirty table cloth. This will ruin the whole dinner. Use place mats if you don't have a good table cloth.
2. Make sure your plates, silverware, and glasses match.
3. All place settings should be the same; there are no variations for left-handed people.
4. A place setting should be set for everyone, even if you know someone will not be eating.
5. As a rule, flatware is placed in the order that it is going to be used from the outside in. For example, the salad fork goes outside of the dinner fork.
6. The crease of the napkin faces the plate.
7. The cutting edge of the knife should point toward the plate.
8. If you have a small table, try putting the place settings a little closer together. The goal of setting a table is to have each place setting look alike.

The Basic Table Setting

I find that the best way to remember things is by word association. When thinking about setting a table think of the word **Funk's** (actually FNKS). This stands for: fork, napkin, knife, spoon.

1. If you are using place mats, the bottom should be an inch away from the edge of the table.
2. The dinner plate goes smack dab in the middle and the bottom should be about two inches away from the edge of the table.
3. The napkin goes on the left side, with the crease facing the plate. Alternately, the napkin may be placed on the center of the plate.
4. The fork goes on top of the napkin, or to the right of it, a half an inch away from the plate.
5. Place the knife (cutting edge in), then the spoon, to the right of the plate. Each utensil should be placed a half an inch away from the plate and each other.
6. The drinking glass is placed two inches above the knife. That's it!

The Formal Place Setting

The reason the formal place setting exists is because you are usually given more food to eat at formal dinners. More food equals more flatware. Each course should have its own utensil. If you are not going to have a certain course, then a utensil is not needed. So if you are not going to have a salad, then don't set the table with a salad fork. The goal of the place setting is to be functional, not to confuse your guests.

1. Start with the basic table setting. Remember only to add the utensils you plan to use.
2. On the left side of the dinner fork put a salad fork.
3. On the right side add a soup spoon.
4. Put the soup bowl two inches above the soup spoon and slightly to the right.
5. The bread plate goes two inches above the fork and to the left. The bread knife goes on top of the bread plate, at a diagonal from upper left to lower right. The serrated edge of the knife should be facing toward you with the handle in the lower right.
6. Salad plates should be placed to the left of the bread plates and about two inches lower.
7. The dessert spoon or fork should be placed an inch above the top of the plate, with the handle facing the right side. If you are using both, the handle of the fork should be facing left and the handle of the spoon facing right.
8. A water glass, the largest on the table, goes two inches above the knife.
9. If you are serving wine then the wine glass should be placed to the right and a little lower than the water glass.

If you go for dinner at your girlfriend's house and can offer to set the table, you will be on good terms with her mom for the rest of your life.

70

How to Make a Bed

When you come home tired from a bad day at work, would you rather flop onto a well-made bed or deal with a pile of unkempt sheets?

There are usually five pieces to making a bed, the pillow, the bottom (or fitted) sheet, the top sheet, a blanket, then the bedspread or comforter. (Some people skip the blanket and just use a comforter.) Most people also have a mattress cover to protect the mattress from getting stained. Unless it's dirty there is no need to launder the mattress cover every time you change the sheets.

Step 1. The Fitted Sheet

After stripping the dirty sheets from your bed, the first thing you have to do is to put on a fitted sheet. Putting on a fitted sheet is like putting on a condom. Awkward, sometimes cumbersome, but it is pretty self-explanatory. However, if you don't know, the four corners of a fitted sheet are elasticized. Put one of these elastic corners on each of the corners of the bed.

Step 2. The Top Sheet

Next you have to put on the top sheet. The reason it is necessary to have a bottom and a top sheet is to make cleaning a little easier. We spend a lot of time in bed, and sheets can get rather dirty. The two sheets are to keep the blankets and comforters from coming into direct contact with our body. This keeps them cleaner, and you have to wash them less.

Standing at one side of the bed, flip the sheet so it billows out and covers the whole mattress. The sides of the sheet should hang evenly. The top edge (which can usually be identified by an elaborate hem), should meet the top of the mattress and the bottom end, where you tuck it in, should hang over about 6–12 inches.

First, tuck the bottom end of the sheet between the box spring and the mattress. Be careful not to pull too much and make the sides uneven. Then do the same to the sides of the sheet, tucking them in between the mattress and box spring. Do this all the way up the sides, but leaving about ½ foot untucked and loose near the top. This is where you will fold over the top sheet and blanket.

Step 3. The Blanket

If you are going to have a blanket on your bed, follow the directions in step 2. (The rule of thumb is that if you have a light bedspread, and not a comforter, a blanket should also be used.)

Step 4. Folding Down the Blanket and the Top Sheet

After tucking in the blanket, grab the top sheet and the blanket with one hand and pull them toward the top of the mattress. This will pull the sheet and blanket tight. Place your other hand on the mattress, about 6 inches down, approximately where you stopped tucking the sheet and blanket into the mattress. Fold the top edge of both the sheet and blanket over the other hand. This will create an even, clean edge. (You will have to do this on both sides of the bed to get an even fold.)

Step 5. The Bedspread

Take the bedspread or comforter, and follow the directions in step 2. The difference with this step is that you do not tuck the sides of the bedspread in between the mattress and box spring. Let them hang down to the floor to cover the sides of the bed frame. Make sure each side is even.

Step 6. Folding Down the Bedspread

To fold down the bedspread, follow the directions in step 4, but fold down the top edge of the bedspread about 2 feet. (You will put the pillows here and should have ample room to cover them.) If you use a comforter, this isn't necessary (or possible) and you should have pillow shams to cover your pillows.

Step 7. Pillows

Take your pillows (don't forget to change your pillow cases) and put them on top of the bedspread that you have just folded over. Fold any excess bedspread over the pillows, then flip the pillows, while holding onto the bedspread, toward the head of the bed. This is a pain and you will have to do this separately to both sides and also straighten them out a few times.

71

How to Do Laundry

Let me be blunt. Doing laundry is a pain in the ass. I hate it. I usually let my laundry pile up for a week or two until I have about six loads and my T-shirts smell like BO. I'm sure that if I didn't let it pile up and did a load every few days, I wouldn't despise it so much. But that would be the practical thing to do, and as we all know, that goes against the natural thinking of man.

What You Will Need

1. Laundry detergent
2. Bleach (optional)
3. Stain pretreatment, like Shout or Wisk (also optional)
4. Fabric softener (optional)
5. A washer and a dryer (not optional)

Step 1. Separating Your Laundry

The first thing you need to do is to separate your laundry into piles: whites, dark colors, light colors, and delicates. Don't wash whites or light colors with dark colors. The dyes in the cloth will run and dye your whites a different color. Dark colors include: jeans, dress socks, and all clothes that are . . . well, dark. Light colors include: pastels, white striped shirts, etc. Whites are white, but are also T-shirts with silk screens on them. Delicates are clothes such as sweaters and dress shirts (and lingerie for you cross dressers). Also, if the label says Dry Clean Only, then have it dry-cleaned—that label is not just a suggestion. (You can also hand-wash the garment in a sink with Woolite or some similar cleaner, but that would be too much work.)

1. If you have a stain, now is a good time to pretreat it. Pretreating a stain increases, but does not guarantee, the likelihood that the stain will come out. (See next chapter.)
2. Wash red clothes or "new" colored clothes separately. They will bleed and discolor your other clothes if you don't. You can test clothes to see if they will bleed by putting a small piece of the clothing in hot water. If the water starts to turn color, then wash it separately. Ever see a guy with a light pink T-shirt?

Step 2. Loading Up the Washer

Take a load and put it into the washer. Make sure that it is evenly distributed. This will prevent the washer basket from getting lopsided, which can cause the newer washers to shut off automatically.

Step 3. Adding Detergent

Add the detergent. Only add the amount of detergent that is recommended on the soap container. For liquid soap, the measuring cup is usually the cap, while powder detergents come with a scoop. Just because you think your clothes are extra dirty, don't add extra soap. Adding extra soap can cause washers to overflow, or the soap to clump up in your clothes. If you are washing a load of whites, add bleach after the washer completely fills with water. Look on the bleach container to determine how much is needed and put it in the bleach dispenser; don't pour it directly on the clothes.

Step 4. Water Settings and Washing Machine Cycles

Set the water temperature. There are two water temperatures for washing clothes. The first is for washing, and the second is for rinsing. Use the following chart:

- **Whites** Hot/Cold
- **Light Colors** Warm/Cold
- **Dark Colors** Warm/Cold or Cold/Cold
- **Delicates** Cold/Cold

Next you have to set the machine wash cycle:

- **Whites** Regular
- **Light Colors** Regular or Permanent Press
- **Dark Colors** Regular or Permanent Press
- **Delicates** Delicate

After the clothes go through the wash cycle, they will be rinsed. Add fabric softener prior to the rinse cycle. Usually a little "rinse" light will come on so you know when to add the fabric softener.

Step 5. Drying Your Clothes

After your clothes have been washed, it is time to dry them, and drying is a lot easier than washing. All you have to do is to take the wash out of the washer, and put it into the dryer (or hang them on a clothes line). Clean the lint filter, set the dial, and push start. With a full load, start the drying time at about 40 minutes. Come back after the first 40 minutes and check to see if they are dry. If not, run it for another 10–20 minutes. Don't dry clothes for too long. They can shrink if overheated, especially vulnerable to high heat is the elastic in socks and underwear. Also, feel around in the dryer and remove any smaller items, such as socks or underwear, that may be dry. Removing the smaller dry items will allow the larger damp items to dry more quickly.

Tips

1. Clothes that are 100 percent cotton may shrink. You may want to hang them up to dry.
2. Make sure you clean out the lint filter. A full lint filter causes the dryer to be less effective, thus taking clothes longer to dry. Also, a full lint filter can catch on fire if the heat is high enough.
3. Add a dryer sheet. Dryer sheets cut down on static electricity. If you use a dryer sheet you don't need to add fabric softener before the rinse cycle.
4. The knob of the washer twists clockwise only. Push the knob in, and turn it to the correct setting. When you are done, pull the knob out to start.
5. The knob of the dryer usually works much the same way. Push in, set, then pull out to activate.
6. Wash and dry towels separately from other garments. They can give off large amounts of lint that can get all over other clothes when washed and dried together.

72

How to Remove a Stain

Sorry, guys, there is no wonder treatment to getting out every stain, and in some cases you will be out of luck no matter what you do. The only practical advice I have is to be conscious of your surroundings and be careful. On the other hand, when you do happen to make a mess, as I have been known to do from time to time, make sure you try to clean it up as soon as possible. Pat or blot with paper towels (don't rub hard on the stain). Here are a few common messes and ways to clean them up:

1. **Coffee** Wet with warm water, wash with an enzyme-based prewash treatment or detergent and rinse. Try to get as much of the stain out as possible, then wash normally, but don't machine

dry until the stain is gone. If it's still there, repeat the prewash and wash steps.

2. **Lipstick** First try to remove the stain with a stain remover (like Shout or other similar commercial product) or you can use denatured wood alcohol. Then apply a prewash stain remover, and rinse. If it won't come out then rub the stain with liquid detergent, and wash in warm water.

3. **Candle wax or crayons** Scrape off as much waxy substance as you can, then put the fabric between two sheets of a paper towel. Use a warm iron which will help to melt the wax out of the fabric. After you have gotten most of the wax out then try an enzyme presoak, or a stain remover. Repeat a few times if necessary. Candle wax is a pain to get out, but it is possible if you get to it quick enough. Another method, especially good for crayons, is to scrape off the excess, spray with WD-40 and let it stand a few minutes. Then work out the crayon wax with a small stiff brush and blot it with paper towels. Rub dishwashing liquid into the area, work it in and wipe stain away with a damp sponge. For tough jobs there is a commercial solvent called Bestine available at office supply stores.

4. **Butter/oil** First use bicarbonate of soda, talcum powder, or cornstarch to absorb as much oil as possible, then rub dishwashing liquid (cuts grease) on the stain, then wash in hot water.

5. **Blood** The best thing to do is to quickly soak the fabric in cold water mixed with salt, then wash with some liquid detergent and rinse in cold water. If the stain is still there, try putting some hydrogen peroxide on the stain for not more than 2–3 minutes. Then rinse with warm water.

6. **Semen** Luckily this comes up with warm water and detergent. You may want to use a pretreatment just to be sure. If you are taking something to the dry cleaners tell them it is raw egg. (They won't believe you, but it will tell them how to get the stain out.)

7. **Alcohol** Alcohol stains are hard to get out. Try rinsing with cold water first. Then soak it for a few minutes in a mixture of warm water, detergent, and a few drops of white vinegar. Then wash in the sink with an enzyme presoak in warm water. For red wine, soak up as much as you can with a paper towel, then sprinkle salt all over the stain. The salt will absorb much of the wine. Wash in cold water, repeat if necessary.

8. **Shoe polish** Just as hard as old alcohol stains. First scrape off as much as you can, then clean the stain with a solution made from

equal parts isopropyl alcohol and water. If it is a white garment, you can use straight alcohol or bleach.

9. **Grass** Soak the fabric in cold water, then rub the stain with isopropyl alcohol. (The alcohol can act like bleach so make sure the fabric can take it first by testing it in a hidden area.) If the stain doesn't come all the way out, soak it in an enzyme presoak for about a half-hour.

10. **Gum** Use ice cubes, or put the piece of clothing in the freezer to harden the gum, then scrape the gum off the fabric. Then use a stain remover to get any leftovers out. (If for some reason you get gum in your hair, try peanut butter. Get a dollop of peanut butter and work it in with the gum. The chemical makeup of the gum and peanut butter interact, and without getting too technical, the gum loosens up considerably so you can pick it out.)

11. **Ink** Dab isopropyl alcohol into the fabric. Then place the fabric, stain side down, on a paper towel. Sponge alcohol onto the stain so it is driven into the paper. Rinse well with warm water and hand-wash in warm water.

12. **Egg** Scrape off as much as you can, then soak in an enzyme presoak and cold water for 15 minutes.

13. **Mud** Let the mud dry, then beat off as much as you can. If a stain is still there, wash by hand with liquid detergent and colorfast bleach. It should come out, and you can wash normally.

14. **Paint (water based)** Make sure you get to paint stains before they dry. Rinse the fabric well with warm water, and hand-wash with liquid detergent. Then apply an enzyme presoak and wash in warm water. Rinse again, then hand-wash. Repeat if necessary.

15. **Paint (oil based)** Scrape off as much as you can (again, do this as soon as possible). Then sponge on some paint thinner, and blot the stain with a paper towel. Repeat. Once you've blotted up as much as you can, rub liquid detergent on the stain while the fabric is still wet with thinner. Hand-wash in hot water.

16. **Rust** Rinse with cool water, then apply a little bit of lemon juice that has been mixed with salt. Boil some water in a pot, then hold the stain over the steam for a few minutes. Rinse thoroughly. (Someone told me this will work, but I have never tried it.)

17. **Fruit juice** Soak immediately in cool water, then wash with an enzyme based presoak. Wait for about twenty minutes, then rinse.

18. **Soft drinks** Rinse the stain in cold water, then dab mixture of equal parts cold water and isopropyl alcohol onto the stain. Apply a prewash treatment and wash as usual.

19. **Ketchup** Wash the stain with a prewash treatment and rinse; then soak in an enzyme presoak for fifteen minutes. Rinse and wash normally.

20. **Vomit** Wet with warm water, sprinkle with baking soda, with an enzyme-based prewash treatment, or detergent and wash and rinse. Try to get as much of the stain out as possible, then wash normally. Make sure you scrub it well, because just the smallest amount of puke can generate one horrendous smell. If it's still there, repeat the prewash and wash steps until the stain and smell are gone.

You may have noticed that you can use an enzyme prewash on a lot of those stains. An enzyme prewash is a solution made of enzymes that you put on stains prior to washing. The enzymes help to break down the chemicals and compounds that make up your stain. The best thing to do is to put one of these on your next grocery list, buy it, and keep it around when you need it. Look at it like car insurance for your clothes—it's there when you have an accident.

If all else fails, take the stained garment to a professional dry cleaner, they can usually get most stains out.

73

How to Iron a Shirt

I feel that ironing a shirt as something a man should only do in an emergency because there is no doubt that shirts look best when they are professionally laundered and pressed. (Also because I can't iron worth a damn.) If you are one of those lucky people who don't have to wear a dress shirt and suit every day, you should still have a few dress shirts professionally cleaned and ready for an emergency. You never know when you will have to go to an important meeting, a date, or even a funeral. On the other hand, if you have to wear a dress shirt every day, then they should always be professionally laundered, and also viewed as disposable. Dress shirts are subject to a lot of wear and tear. Dry-cleaning, spills, and sweat diminish the life span of a shirt. Don't buy a $150 dress shirt, wear it daily, and expect it to last more than six months. I personally prefer 100 percent cotton shirts because I like their texture and they look best when pressed. On the other hand, cotton has a shorter life span, and stains don't come out of it very easily. For everyday wear I recommend shirts made of a cotton-polyester blend. They don't look like a rag at the end of a hot and humid day, and sometimes you can wear them more than once, before you have to have them dry-cleaned. Dry-cleaning can get damned expensive.

Step 1. The first thing you have to do is to set up the ironing board and the iron. Make sure you have plenty of space to move around the entire board, and enough cord for the iron to reach around the whole board too.

Step 2. If the iron has steam capabilities, now is a good time to fill up the steam vent (prior to plugging it in of course). Next plug in the iron, and set it to the appropriate fabric setting. If an iron is set too high for a fabric then the fabric will burn and the shirt will be ruined. Check the shirt tag to determine the type of fabric and set accordingly. While you are letting the iron heat up make sure it is standing upright.

Step 3. After waiting a few minutes to let the iron warm up, check it to see if it is hot. Never touch an iron that you think is hot. The best way to check it is to flick some water on it (no, it is not OK to spit on it). If it sizzles it is hot and ready. If your shirt is badly wrinkled then you may want to use some spray starch. Spray the shirt a section at a time, not all at once.

Step 4. The best way to iron a shirt is in sections. Start with the yoke and collar. If it is a button down, unbutton it and fold it up, ironing it flat against the board, not against the shirt. Go on to the sleeves, the sides and the back, and finally the front.

There is no real trick except time, patience, and experience. However, you may want to pay extra attention to seams, and use spray starch. They are usually the hardest part of a shirt to iron.

Step 5. When you are done, hang the shirt on a hanger; don't put it on the back of a chair or over a door until you are ready to wear it. Shut off the iron, and let it cool down. Never put away a hot iron. (I don't need to explain that, do I?) It should take about 15–20 minutes to cool down. Later, put away the ironing board and the iron.

74

How to Shine Your Shoes

Even though a man will look you in the eye when he talks to you, he only needs half a second to glance down at your shoes. An Armani suit, a $100 haircut, and even fresh breath will be overlooked if you have scuffed, unshined shoes. Everybody, especially women, notices shoes. One of my female friends who works at an advertising agency was in the process of hiring someone to fill a graphic design position at her office. We were talking one night after work and she said it was a toss-up between these two talented guys. They were equally qualified, and she said she wanted them both. A few days later I was talking to her again and she told me that she had made a decision: she had hired the guy with the nicely shined shoes. She said that it gave her the impression that he took pride in himself and paid attention to details. This, of course, made me think that I am glad that I don't work with my neurotic friend.

What You Will Need

1. Saddle soap
2. Polish
3. A soft polishing cloth or brush
4. A soft buffing cloth

The first step is to wash your shoes with saddle soap. (You wash your car before you wax it, don't you?) Second, apply a small amount of polish to the cloth or brush and apply it to your shoes in a circular motion. Make sure you work it into each crack and crevasse. After working the whole shoe, set it aside to let the polish dry a little. After a few minutes, buff the shoe with a soft cloth until the polish has been completely worked into the shoe. This should be repeated weekly. For a high-gloss shine you can dip cotton balls into water and then into the polish. Polish the shoe with this combination, buff, then add more water, and buff again. This is known as a "spit shine." Easier still is the use of a silicon sponge over the polished shoes that gives a high-gloss shine.

When not on your feet, shoes should be kept on shoe trees. If you don't use shoe trees then just go ahead and rip this page out of the book, because nothing can fix a shoe with a broken sole, even a good shine. The trees help to keep the shoes' shape, and prevents them from curling at the ends.

Shoe Rules

1. Your belt and shoes should match in color.
2. *Always* wear socks: foot sweat causes fungus. Fungus causes shoe leather to break down, athletes foot, and stinky feet.
3. A good pair of shoes, if properly cared for, will last you the rest of your life.
4. *Always* use shoe trees. I cannot overemphasize this.

75

How to Wrap a Gift

I like giving gifts as much as the next guy, but what I hate is that I have to wrap them. It seems like such a waste to wrap a present in paper that is just going to be thrown away. I wrap a present and an hour later all my hard work is in the trash can. I shared my opinion with my wife one time and she told me that a wrapped gift is extra special since you took the time to wrap it yourself. After she shared her thoughts with me, I asked her what I got her on her last birthday. She answered correctly. I then asked her how the package was wrapped. She couldn't remember.

What You Will Need

1. A package to wrap
2. Wrapping paper
3. Scotch tape (Scotch tape is the clear tape)
4. Scissors
5. Some ribbon and bows
6. Patience and time

Step 1. Measure and Cut

The thing that frustrates me the most is when I don't measure the dimensions of the gift I am going to wrap and I cut the paper too small. The width of the paper should be *double the width of the box*. The length of the wrapping paper should equal the *circumference of the box. (The total measure-ment of all four sides + 2 inches of wrapping paper.)*

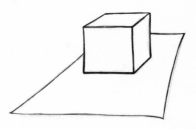

Step 2. Wrapping the Box

Wrap the wrapping paper around the box. Tape one side of the paper directly to the box then pull the other side to get rid of any slack in the paper. To create a clean edge that you will tape directly to the gift wrap, fold over a half inch of wrapping paper then proceed to tape it into place. The clean folded edge will hide the fact that you may not be the best at cutting a straight line with scissors.

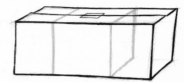

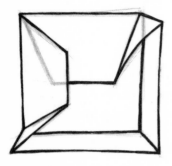

Step 3. Folding the Sides

The next, and possibly the most difficult, is folding over the sides of the wrapping paper and also making it look presentable. Start with the top of the box. Fold down the edge of the wrapping paper that is covering the top of your gift box. Tape it into place. Next crease the sides of the paper, fold them into place, and tape. End by folding and taping the bottom. Follow the same directions for the other side.

Step 4. Ribbons and Bows

Once you have gone through all the trouble of wrapping a gift you might as well spend the time to add a ribbon and bow. Measure out a length of ribbon that is about two and a half times the size of the gift. This should give you enough length. First wrap it around one side of the box and tie it into place with a simple overhand knot. (This knot is the one used in the first step of tying your shoe.) Here is the tricky part: once you have tied that knot, turn the ribbon so you can wrap it around the other side of the box. Wrap it around and tie it into place. At this point, you can either tie your own bow, or put a store-bought preassembled one on top. Now you can present your gift so the recipient can destroy what you have just created.

Tips

1. If you are going to spend the time wrapping a present, spend the money on wrapping paper of a good quality and weight. The cheaper papers will rip easily.
2. Try to tie your own bow, an imperfect bow that you have tied yourself will mean more than a store-bought one that you have slapped on top.
3. If you are wrapping several gifts at once, don't forget to add name tags. Believe me it is easy to forget who gets which gift. You don't want to give your dad the underwear you got for your girlfriend.
4. Give gifts that may be viewed as personal, like sexy underwear or lingerie, in private. Your girlfriend will appreciate the new teddy you bought for her, but I doubt her father will.

76

How to Balance a Checkbook

Balancing a checkbook is a black and white issue. You are either the type of person that balances your checkbook or you are not. I personally am one of those people that always has to know how much I have in my account and don't understand why some people just don't care. Just in case you were wondering, balancing your checkbook is not the same as keeping a daily balance. Balancing your checkbook when you get your monthly statement is more accurate, because it includes fees and interest earned that may not be taken into consideration when keeping your daily balance. If you don't balance your checkbook regularly then it is possible that a forgotten $.50 ATM fee can overdraw your account. Fortunately, balancing your checkbook is pretty easy, the only thing you really need is the time and the desire to do it.

Step 1. Record All Your Transactions

This step is the most important because if you don't write down every transaction, then it is impossible to know where to start. Make sure you record everything.

1. ATM withdrawals
2. ATM fees (Your bank and the ATM you use can charge fees.)
3. Point-of-sale transactions
4. Automatic payments and deposits
5. Transfers
6. Deposits
7. Withdrawals
8. Checks
9. Bank fees
10. Earned interest

Step 2. Checking Your Checkbook

When you get your statement, compare it with your checkbook register. Put a check by the transactions that appear on your statement.

Step 3. Transactions That Have Not Cleared

On the back of bank statements there is a form that is there to help you balance your checkbook. On the top of that form write down the balance that you currently have in your *checkbook*. Compare your statement and your checkbook register, and under the checkbook balance write down all the checks that have *not* cleared your account. (These will be the ones that will *not be on your statement.*) *Add* them to your checkbook balance. After adding checks that have not cleared, *subtract* any deposits that have not cleared.

Step 4. Matching Your Numbers

After adding checks and subtracting deposit to the balance listed in your checkbook register, the number you end up with should match with the ending balance on your statement. If it does not, go back and double check your math. If you still can't find your error, then go back and make sure you have properly accounted for all of your transactions.

Hints to Finding Errors

1. If the difference between the statement and the checkbook register can be divisible by two, then you may have added when you should have subtracted, or vice versa.
2. If the difference is divisible by nine this may indicate that you transposed numbers when recording a transaction. Example: $12 instead of $21.

INDEX